Words to Paint With

Words to Paint With

a collection of prose & poetry

Salt Lake City, Utah

WORDS TO PAINT WITH
a collection of prose & poetry

ISBN-13: 978-0988236707
ISBN-10: 0988236702

Cover design and book formatting by Mark E. Moody. This book uses Kaushan Script by Pablo Impallari, IM Fell Flowers 1, and IM Fell Flowers 2 by Igino Marini, all licensed under the SIL Open Font License, 1.1 at http://scripts.sil.org/OFL.
Photograph resources from www.morgueFile.com used under the morgueFile license by the following contributors: mirabbi, Irish_Eyes, juben, and Kevin Schnaper/Ferrara 2003.

CONTENTS

ONE-OH-FIVE

Chadd VanZanten

About three quarters of the way through our first road trip to California, somewhere in Arizona I guess, I noticed Dad sitting a little taller in the driver's seat and driving with a certain extra swagger. I was only nine, but it was clear even to me that he was getting ready to make a point.

My older brother Marshall slouched next to me in the back seat, dozing with the car's rocking. The travel compass on the dash spun through all four points as Dad steered into a big new cloverleaf just outside Flagstaff.

When we reached highway speed, which in those days was 55 miles per hour, Dad said, "All right, everyone. Look at this."

Marshall jerked awake and we both leaned forward, hunching on the backrest of the front seat to see out the windshield. Dad made a sweeping gesture at something ahead.

"Look," he breathed.

A sunny expanse of Interstate stretched into the distance before us. Nothing more.

"Oh, great," Marshall sneered. "A road."

Mom looked up from her magazine for a couple seconds, then looked down again.

Some people say the journey is more important than the destination, and there's some truth to it, but in my family it was just a way to hide what we were all usually thinking: "We drove all this way—to see that?"

My dad felt the destination really was irrelevant. He worked for the Federal Highway Administration, and he may have married my mom, but his first love was the U.S. Interstate Highway System. In our family vacation photos, Dad can usually be seen fiddling with his road map, thinking of the next on-ramp.

It would be inaccurate to say that we traveled *to* every state, but it felt like we had at least gone *through* them all. Dad's objective was to drive every mile of U.S. Interstate, so where the highways ended was immaterial—to him there was no difference between a pricey suite in a Marriot Hotel with a view of Disneyland, and a funny-smelling Motel 8 in Squankum, New Jersey. The road was the vacation; the journey was the destination.

"No, Marshall, this is not just any road. This is Route 66," announced Dad, a little too loudly. "Just like in the song."

"What song?" said Marshall.

"You know, Chicago to L.A., get your kicks on Route 66."

"Sign says I-40."

"Sure, they call it I-40 now, but originally it was Route 66. Same road. You take away a couple inches of asphalt and maybe some sub-bed—same road. Now. Isn't that something?"

He searched our faces in the rearview mirror.

"Boys, this is it," he persisted. "The Will Rogers Highway. This is where it all begins."

I wanted to feel something. I looked out the windows, but I guess the Flagstaff stretch of Route 66 was careful about giving up her secrets that day. Marshall and I slumped back into our seat.

The light-blue Ford station wagon my family rode throughout the 1970s and almost all the way through the 80s was nicknamed "the Staish." Blisters of rust were developing low on her fenders and the electric windows groaned alarmingly when activated, but the Staish always struck me as quite sleek, with lots of chrome inside and out. The rear bumper was a collage of decals from fuel stations and souvenir shops.

If you were to describe the Staish as "roomy," it would be an open insult to the Ford Motor Company. "Cavernous" is probably the word they had in mind. The bench seats were wide enough to accommodate a modest religious congregation, serve potluck dinner on the dashboard after benediction.

Marshall had once asked, "Why's it called a station wagon? It's not a station, and it's not a wagon."

Dad always had an answer for questions like this. "Station wagons were invented to pick up people from the train station, Marsh," he said. "The people ride up front and the luggage goes in the back."

By the "back" Dad meant the place we called the "back-back," a cargo area behind the back seat, but we never kept luggage there. Dad lashed our bags to the roof rack with yards of nylon rope. This left the back-back free for us to roam around. There was even a backwards-facing rumbleseat, which we pretended was the tailgun of a B-17. Dad never drove very fast, so when cars passed us by, Marshall and I would let them have it like they were enemy Zeros.

Dad was quiet but intent as the Staish rolled on down Route 66 for a few miles, but soon he pointed through the windshield again.

"Okay, you guys," he said. "Look at this."

Marshall and I pulled ourselves back up, more slowly this time. The same highway stretched into the distance, only now it climbed a hill and bent to the right.

"Curve coming up," said Dad. "And an overpass after that. See the curve up ahead? But it tilts, too. See the tilt? Just a coupla degrees—like that." He held up his hand at a slight angle.

I squinted at the bend in the highway, but it was as yet a few miles off yet.

"Ever notice how racetracks are banked on the curves?" Dad continued. "Same thing on these highways. That's why we can do sixty all the way through and not even feel it. If it was flat, like they were years ago, we'd have to slow down to forty or forty-five. Now. Isn't that something?"

Marshall sighed and let his face fall into his hands. I read Dad's expression in the mirror and knew he wasn't done.

"Don'tcha see?" he said. "It's American Ingenuity right in front of you. Without that tilt, we'd go flying off the road. We'd fly right off, like a— like a—"

But he couldn't think of anything, so he trailed off and stared out the windshield, his face coloring.

Marshall, maybe feeling guilty, halfheartedly offered help. "Like a helicopter?"

"No," said Dad testily, "not like a helicopter."

"Like a jet," I corrected, thinking he was looking for a simile with more horsepower, more velocity.

"No, we wouldn't take flight. We'd just fly off the embankment and crash."

"A helicopter could crash," contended Marshall.

Dad clicked his tongue and sighed.

"Like a missile, Howard," Mom suggested, without looking up. "We'd fly off like a missile."

"Well, okay, maybe," said Dad. "That's a little better. Better than a helicopter, anyhow."

Marshall was fond of helicopters. He glared at Dad. "What's so bad about helicopters?"

"Marsh, it's not about that. It's about the road design, it's about the engineering. Just look at that tilt. Forget sixty. The design speed is probably ninety—we could do a hundred all the way through."

Marshall and I looked at each other. Marshall's expression seemed to say, "Finally, something to work with."

"Can we?" Marshall asked, but it was no question. It was a challenge.

"No," said Mom, flipping a page.

We did not see Dad's foot press down on the gas, but the long needle of the speedometer stirred and then proceeded steadily right, through the sixties and into the seventies. Mom snapped her magazine shut.

"Howard, no," she said.

"Floor it, Dad," said Marshall.

Dad's eyes narrowed in the mirror as Marshall and I leaned forward. The engine revved hoarsely, and there was another sound above us. Dad always covered the luggage in the roof rack with a blue tarp in case of thunderstorms. A flap of it must have worked loose because as we gained speed it crackled loudly sound, like machinegun fire.

Mom clutched at the dashboard; the magazine spilled from her lap.

"Howard," she warned.

The Staish shot past a gently bouncing U-Haul van, put on some more steam, then zipped by a red sports car, something that had never happened before.

"That was a 280z!" cried Marshall, turning and pointing as the car fell behind us.

When the speedometer needle pushed up through eighty, the Staish began to shudder. We overtook a Lincoln Continental, but now we were climbing the hill. The old engine struggled against gravity, and the curve was coming on fast.

"Come on," growled Dad. He looked down at the speedometer, not to see how fast we were going, but to address the Staish more personally, more directly. "Come on, baby."

As the Staish rocketed into the turn, we were pulled toward the driver's side with surprising force. Dad had started out with only his left hand on the steering wheel. Now he perhaps thought it would be a show of weakness to bring his right hand into play, and so the sinews in his skinny forearm stood out as he worked one-handed to stay on the road. The Staish strained to swerve straight, cross oncoming traffic, and plow through the guardrail, and I wondered what it would be like when it did—helicopter, jet, or missile.

"Marshall, Nathan," Dad muttered. "Maybe you boys oughta buckle up."

The Staish was fitted with heavy straps that met the technical specification of seat belts, but we used them so infrequently they had worked down into the upholstery and were hard to find. Automobile crash safety had yet to catch on in those days; seat belts were for astronauts and racecar drivers. Passenger car designers seemed more concerned with figuring out all the different places where little chrome ashtrays could be placed. The seat belts were primarily used as restraining devices for when Marshall and I misbehaved.

Mom placed her hand lightly on Dad's arm, not to stop him or even slow him down, but maybe for the same reason someone on a doomed airliner reaches out to a fellow passenger just before impact. Dad took this for a signal that the situation was deteriorating, brushed off Mom's touch, and took the wheel in both hands. The muscles in his jaw pulsed and his eyes gleamed as though he were contemplating the age of the car's Firestones, or the integrity of the rack and pinion, or the half-dozen other components that might choose that moment to fail.

Centripetal force pulled harder as we hit ninety. Mom slid halfway across the bench seat and listed so deeply it looked like she was searching for something in the ashtray. Marshall and I gripped the seatback furiously to avoid slipping down behind the driver's seat, but our eyes darted from the road to the speedometer and back.

Marshall shouted, "Faster, faster, faster," but we could scarcely hear him over the engine sound, howling tires, and the sharp sputtering of the tarp overhead.

The Staish bucked and shook like a space capsule re-entering Earth's atmosphere. Dad had abandoned any façade of fatherly composure—the car was now driving him and he knew it. He wore a bare-teeth, test-pilot grimace as he fought the car yard by yard until at last the speedometer needle touched the 100 mile-per-hour hashmark.

I knew cars could go that fast, if only in theory. At the speedway we'd seen dragsters go over 200 miles per hour. Even the speedometer in the Staish went to 120, but no one ever knew Dad to go faster than 70. He had done so only once, to race to the hospital after Grandma Sweet had her stroke. I had always assumed 70 was the Staish's top speed and that the numbers to the right were merely to fill up unused space and add symmetry to the instrument panel. Now the needle trembled over the 100 mark and I thought surely the car would propel ahead or backward in time, or at least into another dimension.

Marshall hollered, "One hundred, one hundred, one hundred!"

Mom whimpered, "Howard, enough."

Dad did not slow down.

The hypothesis was that American Ingenuity enabled us to not only reach 100, but maintain it through the turn. Dad knew the exact point where Route 66 returned to a straightaway, but he dared not cheat American Ingenuity out of one single degree of the curve, so he kept the hammer down for another two hundred yards just to be sure. I could hang on no longer. When I let go of the seatback, I knocked Marshall off, too, and we fell together behind the driver's seat.

In the split second before I tumbled down, I saw the speedometer read one-oh-five.

Only then the engine's blast and the squall of tires receded. The blue tarp on the luggage was reduced to an occasional flapping. The car's transmission eased out of overdrive and, eventually, so did Dad. He took a few deep breaths, and then grinned.

"Like a meteor," he said. "We'd fly off like a meteor."

I heard my mother retrieve her magazine and scoot back to the passenger side.

"Howard," she said. "Just. Drive. The car."

Marshall and I lay in a heap where we had fallen behind Dad's seat. The Staish had not shifted in time or dimension, but in me ignited a new awareness, not only to the physical world, but to the universe of what is possible. Marshall laughed and cheered as he climbed up to his place on the bench seat. I arose cautiously, as though when I looked through the windshield again, everything would be completely different.

It was.

TREASURES

"I found a garage sale!" he called from his truck,
then carried his box up, amazed with his luck,
a kid with a puppy, a Cracker Jack toy.
The man was elated, a "Happy Meal" boy.
"A dollar," he bragged, "For the whole wooden crate."
I quietly questioned the mind of my mate.
He dropped his pirate chest at my feet,
a cave man, a hunter, home with the meat.
"The whole box," he said, quite simply aglow.
"I knew it was worth it." *Now how did he know?*
I glanced at the junk, broken mugs and a plate.
He pulled out a coaster. "Isn't it great?"
"Look through it," he urged. "What can you use?"
"Such a marvelous bargain, you've nothing to lose."
Just my time, I decided, *my time and my day,*
I wasn't intending to waste it this way.
"This is somebody's garbage!" I started to shout.
"Why were they frightened to just throw it out?"
A lint brush, a button, a bangle, a shoe,
nothing unbroken, let alone new.
Then down in the bottom I found something cool.
Like a plastic crochet hook, an orange peeling tool.
Mom had one once. It worked like a dream.
But they made them no more, or so it would seem.
This thing is perfect to take off a rind.
"The whole box for a dollar?" What a wonderful find.

—Caren Leibelt

11

NEVER FORGOTTEN

Emily Younker

Captain Ivan was a mighty pirate bounty hunter. Sometimes it was difficult to juggle both careers, but it was most definitely worth it. He told the men they were in it for the bounty booty, but that wasn't entirely true. No one talked about the reason why Ivan was both pirate and bounty hunter.

His crew currently consisted of three people, not including himself, and he was hoping to recruit a few more soon. As Ivan and his men docked a great noise thundered.

"Evan, time for dinner."

Sighing, Evan carefully set the four little Lego men in the small box that served as a boat and folded the blue blanket. When everything was neat, he climbed up the flight of stairs to the dining room.

"Do you want me to call Tommy?" Mother asked, keeping her hands busy and not looking at Evan as he slid into a chair.

Evan knew he shouldn't spend as much time in the basement, but school was out for Christmas. Without school as a distraction, he didn't like to be around other kids unnecessarily. All he needed was to think of Jim and play with the Legos.

After dinner, the table clean and dishes done, he was back downstairs spreading the blanket on the floor and positioning the boat.

After removing the Jolly Roger, so as not to alarm anyone, Captain Ivan docked at the nearest town. Leaving the crew to watch the ship, he meandered innocently to the police station. A man, who looked identical to one of the crew members, handed Ivan a list of available bounties. After looking it over, Ivan went back to the ship. There was no sense in plundering the town; he wouldn't get the bounty if he did.

They sailed around to another port. Ivan signaled for two crew members to join with him on the hunt. As they disembarked, a giant's shadow covered the land.

"Evan, I just saw a group of boys headed to the field. Do you want to go?"

Irritated at being disturbed, Evan shook his head then remained still until mother left.

At the top of the stairs she called down, "Don't forget to clean everything up when you're done. You know how much your father hates to find your Legos with his feet."

With the shadow finally gone, Ivan and the crew breathed a sigh of relief. Giants were unpredictable. There were times they had to hide for a while so the giants wouldn't find them. Ivan and the two crewmen journeyed inland. There was a small village and, brandishing cutlasses, they attacked. They were in luck since they found several gold bricks.

As they headed back to the ship, they met a man on the road. His appearance matched the description of the bounty. Ivan tied him up and dragged him back to the ship, pleased with the good fortune. The bounty would remain locked in the hold until turned over to the authorities. Ivan made sure the crew and the bounty were separated. One crew member and the bounty were identical, and it would be awkward if they were related.

Back at the first town, Ivan received two gold bricks for the captured man. Ivan was always paid in gold bricks, and he had almost all of them in the whole world. He absently wondered how he would be paid when he had all the gold.

Since it had been a good day, Ivan docked the boat in the secret port until the call of adventure stirred again.

After cleaning everything up, Evan left the basement. It was getting late and he didn't want his family to know where the Legos were hidden. He always hid them before anyone announced that it was time for bed. Loud voices drifted through the door at the top of the stairs, and Evan paused to listen. There were often loud voices when his parents thought no one was listening.

"He's got to get out. Boys should be playing with friends."

Mother's patient voice was taught. "Evan will do what he wants."

"Taking away the Legos will improve everything. You aren't planning on buying him any for Christmas, are you?"

"Have you seen him play? With only four it's a little difficult."

"He would have five if he hadn't buried one. That was irresponsible and shouldn't be encouraged."

There was a pause then Father added, "Did you see the career choice paper from school? He wants to be a pirate bounty hunter."

"He's nine. Anything is still possible," Mother reasoned.

"He's not getting any better; last year he only wanted to be a bounty hunter."

Evan was tired and the argument depressed him. He silently moved down a few stairs and then stomped back up. There was no sign of contention as he walked into the room. He kissed Mother good night and as he headed to bed, Father grumbled.

"Doesn't even say goodnight."

"Hush."

"James is dead. Remaining silent won't help."

Evan shut the door to his bedroom and ignored the empty bed. There was no other place to put it. With misty eyes, he gazed at the walls covered with papers. One drawing showed two people, one with an eye patch, the other carried rope. Another picture showed one man with rope and eye patch. Written in a shaky hand under it was: Never forgotten.

Tomorrow, he promised, tomorrow he would talk. Captain Jim would want him to. There were other ways to remember Jim.

KARMIC BURDEN

She wipes the child's nose and bottom,
stitches the torn coat, stirs the mush,
trims the bangs, tapes the knee and
knots the coin in the hanky's corner.
She wrings the nubby cloth from the dish
and cools the fevered cheek.
She sweeps the corners, labors over homework
and fashions the prom dress.
Her anxious prayers hang like winter smoke as she
paces the worn carpet in the predawn hours.

She resists the tug of eons that constantly
nudge the edges of this lifetime as she
strains to believe that, this time, love will flow
with its cleansing resolution—
but it does not.
Karma, cruel in its lack of explanation
relentlessly points to a new day—
a day gone suddenly bright and sharp as a knifed edge.

—Betty J. Vickers

RIVER ROOTS

Marie Tollstrup

Mom tiptoed around Dad lying on the couch. She looked like a ballerina balancing swimsuits and towels in both hands. "Swimming, anyone?" she whispered. Mom succeeded in not waking Dad, whose fog-horn snore told us we were still safe. We wanted to avoid an extension of his Sunday morning black mood, which had dashed our spirits.

Hearing Mom's invitation, my smile grew. Sweeping up my long brown hair, I twisted it on the crown of my head and secured it with three bobby pins.

Our goal—side-step Mom and Dad's adversarial relationship. Dad sparred about anything, just to hear his own voice drown out Mom's position. Their cacophonous voices, the norm in our house, argued the minutest details. "You *can* raise pumpkins in the garden? We live on a damn farm, don't we?" Dad's salvos landed around us in a constant barrage. One fight down, and another flared up without warning.

Just the prospect of wading in the river chased my depression away. "Whoever wants to go, swimsuits on now." Mom's command motivated us because we had an affinity for the river's tranquility. In a flurry of color, we donned our suits. Because Jeanne, the youngest of our clan, still struggled to fasten her yellow flowered suit, I knelt down to help her.

Indian style we sneaked out the family room to the porch and down the worn steps. The screen door banged when Roger lost his grip on the screen while clutching an inner tube.

"Where are you guys going?"

Dad's voice burrowed into my heart. Now we're in for it, I figured.

Mom stopped in her tracks, retreated, and stuck her head back into the house. "We're going swimming."

"You're always gallivanting," Dad accused. "I want my supper on time."

"Not a problem." I admired Mom for being cool and not backing down. I didn't want to witness another pointless argument like the one on our drive to church. Mom quietly did what she thought was best for us kids.

The mid-afternoon May sun seeped into our skins as we walked in its warm caress. How lucky to open the season with a warm swim. Bernie challenged, "Let's explore farther upstream."

"Fine, but I have to be near the river's edge to see your five heads," Mom said, power in her voice. The river had become our ally. We learned how to swim its currents and bonded with the river's constant well of healing, rooted in its therapeutic powers.

I looked back at the house for fear Dad would change his mind and order us back home. Why didn't he ever come with us? Relieved, I saw no one appear on the porch.

We continued our trek on the short-cut diagonal road that cut through the field down to the Red River bordering Grandpa's farm. The river sliced the neighbor's land from Grandpa's which rose up to meet River Road. We looked like gypsies, decked out in pink, yellow, blue, and red, swimsuits being our favorite costumes.

"I love the current carrying me," Pat said, her blond head bobbing while she walked.

"I'll race you, Pat," I said, daring her as I swayed from side to side.

"Who cares who swims the fastest," Mom said flatly. Her hands punctuated her words. "What's important, you're learning to swim."

Two birds playing tag swooped down in front of us. I looked up into the expanse of blue sky, peppered with wispy, floating clouds. The wind's embrace carried us without effort.

"Remember, be careful playing in the river," Mom warned as she readjusted towels on her shoulder. "I wish I learned to swim when I was a kid."

I thought, how's it possible Mom doesn't know how to swim?

Mom interrupted my reverie. "I wasn't afraid of water, but we couldn't visit the river often. Grandma was afraid we'd drown, so she didn't encourage our learning to swim." Mom looked back at the big house, defiance alive in her eyes. "In fact, Grandma wouldn't let us girls wade any deeper than our ankles! Try learning to swim with that restriction."

I felt sorry for Mom. I craned my neck to see her face and noted a far-away, sad expression. "But my children will learn to swim."

"How about swimming in The Pond?" Bernie asked, squinting into the sun, his tousled brown hair in his eyes.

Phlox's large reservoir formed, damming up the Red River for the town's hydro-plant. The Pond was *the* premier swimming spot, featuring an anchored raft with an attached diving board. A small island jutted out into The Pond some distance from the sandy entry point. My dream was to swim to this enchanted island.

"That's my plan." Mom looked around and checked to see if five heads were still visible in her bevy. "You'll get your wish once you learn to swim in the river. The Pond is deep and dangerous."

Bernie smiled broadly. He knew Mom kept her word.

We crested the hill. What a view, spreading as far as the eye could see. The fringe of trees bordering the river touched the sky. We spotted a few cows off in the distance. Their large, red-orange splotched bodies moved gracefully and meandered in the paths they had created through the trees. The close-cropped grassy hills, manicured by the cows, sloped gradually down to the river's edge. Grandpa loved Guernsey cows, and was known in Wisconsin for his healthy, pure-bred herd.

I thought, how could Dad and Grandpa be so different? Dad was like rain to Grandpa's sunshine. Dad never got close to any cows, preferring his potato fields. I shook my head and wiped the comparison from my mind as we moved closer to the spreading idyllic scene.

While playing tag, we chased and shoved each other, stumbling over large rocks in the road. "You're it, Shirley!" Pat screamed and swiped my red polka-dotted, one-piece suit. I took after Jeanne, who was within my reach, and tried to tag her yellow flowered suit.

"Be careful not to fall," Mom said.

Tall, blue-green grass fringed either side of the path down the slope. Roger reached out and plucked a strand of grass. He began to suck on the sweet, tender stalk that had been protected by its outer sheath. I followed suit. It tasted like the baby lettuce we grew in our garden. When I looked around, we all had become Roger's copycat, enjoying the pleasing marrow of grass stalks. I chuckled. We pretended to smoke long elegant cigarettes.

Nearing the Red River's edge, we heard its steady, gurgling current. I never grew tired of the river's rushing melody. The music soothed my inner being and calmed my turmoil. We raced the last stretch of the grassy slope to see who would get wet first.

"Wade in the shallow part of the river near those large boulders," Mom said, her arm outstretched. "That way I can rest and watch you." The sun's reflection revealed the dimpled river's surface. The moving, transparent current revealed varied colored pebbles, sand, impeding rocks, algae, and driftwood covering the riverbed. I studied small schools of fish, making their way up stream. A large rainbow trout darted right in front of me and brushed my leg. "Did you see that big trout?"

"Oh, it's cold!" Jeanne squealed. She had entered the river where a large tree shaded the water.

"Come over here to a warmer spot," Mom said. She perched herself on a large rock that jutted out of the river's base. The rock's surface was flat, offering a seat to those who braved the stream and reached its comfort. Mom took off her shoes and bathed her feet in the shallow water warmed by the sun. She looked young because the wrinkles between her eyes had vanished. Mom threw her head back and sported a broad grin.

I was relieved to see her this way. Mom and Dad's feisty words had rallied back and forth in the car both coming and going to church that morning. Would they ever be on the same side? Who cared when we would go see Dad's parents? When we did, Dad and his family spoke Bohemian, a language that cut Mom and us off from Dad's family. So why were we so-called *visiting* Grandpa and Grandma?

It was beyond my comprehension why they fought on Sunday, the day we went to church to visit God. Dad, who professed a deep religious faith, totally ignored its main tenet, love one another, especially his family. This irritated me for years. His harsh, argumentative words wounded us all, especially Mom. Here, listening to the river's soothing current, it was different. The river washed away his brutal words while we were distracted and had fun.

I re-tested the water with my foot and pulled it to safety. Then I regained my courage and joined Bernie and Roger, who splashed water at one another midstream. I held my breath as I stepped into the river's edge. The chocolate silt, murky and silky, squished between my toes. Soon after, I ventured out further, where pebbles, stones, and shells made it difficult to walk. We searched for the variegated green algae patches that became carpets for our bruised feet. The water, a clear sheet of glass, made this quest easy.

Acclimated to the cold, surging water, we made our way upstream in search of our premier swimming hole. At one point where the river narrowed, trees on both sides of the river reached their arms over the stream and formed a natural canopy. I felt protected, trees and river together forming a private wading pool, a perfect place to regain serenity. A sudden breeze soothed my body.

Near the bank we had just climbed, the riverbed had been conveniently scooped out and left a permanent water depth reaching up to our waists. Because it was on the side of the river, the current was not as swift as mid-stream, a good spot to attempt our virgin dog paddling. We forged upstream beyond our swimming hole, where it was easier to swim with the current that carried us in its embrace.

The water gently swirled around my shoulders as I stroked the water with my arms, fluttered my legs, keeping my head barely above the chilled water's surface. "Next time let's swim together, Pat," I suggested, brushing the hair out of my eyes.

"Our race is on." Pat loved a challenge.

"I'll beat the winner," Bernie yelled, splashing Roger with plumes of water by slapping the river's surface. Roger cut around Bernie's back and returned fire. Both their bodies were slicked with water. Bernie grabbed Roger's arm behind his back and submerged him in the river. Roger squirmed out of his grip and escaped.

Jeanne stayed clear of both of the water fights and races. She found a shallow part of the river to test her skills. In the distance Mom craned her neck to count five heads, her full-time job.

Two cows made their way down to the river's edge to get a drink. A third was chewing her cud.

"Where's Jeanne?" Mom's question alarmed us. We stopped dead. "I just saw her a second ago!" Mom's high pitched voice cut through me.

We thrashed around the water and searched. "How could she disappear that fast?" My breath came in shallow spurts. Mom waded toward us and fought the brisk stream, arms flailing, eyes frantic. The wind suddenly gusted through the trees, hugging the river banks, and swept a rippled path over the water. Our idyllic world had become a seething stage, one fraught with danger.

Together we spotted Jeanne. Behind an imposing rock midstream, the river's face swirled over Jeanne's head. I lunged through the current, but Pat was closer. She snatched her out of the water but fell as she tried to rescue Jeanne. Both Pat and Jeanne thrashed in the stream. I was close enough to grab Jeanne's hand and kept her head above water.

Roger, right behind me, hoisted Jeanne in his arms, and carried her to safety on the grassy shore. In the process his right foot squished a fresh cow pie. Jeanne's hacking cough made me realize she had swallowed a lot of water. Mom's ample body moved swiftly, thrusting forward, intent on her purpose. She scooped Jeanne out of Roger's arms. He hobbled off to wash the clinging manure by dangling his foot in a river eddy close to shore. Because Roger was off-balance, Bernie pushed him into the river.

Mom bent over Jeanne to check her breathing. It was a moment that put us on alert. Mom's arms enfolded Jeanne and cradled her petite body to soothe her. "See why you have to look out for each other?" Mom warned while stroking Jeanne's curly black hair away from her face. I read fear in Mom's eyes, large and midnight, and studied her solemn face. We circled Mom and Jeanne like a wolf pack, hardly breathing, and waited for Mom's pronouncement.

"God bless you kids." Mom's voice faltered. "You saved Jeanne's life." Her weak smile showed some relief. "Swim a bit longer. Then we'll start for home." Mom turned to Bernie. "Stop picking on Roger."

Mom was fair and saw everything. She was cautious, but not in the extreme. She rode crises better than anyone I knew. She had that quality of being level-headed and cool, not hysterical and overly dramatic.

"But, Mom, you said we could explore more of the river," Bernie whined while he stirred a steaming cow pie with a stick.

"You'll simply have to wait," Mom said. "Besides, this river's not going anywhere." She freed her right hand still cuddling Jeanne and swept it towards the fields and river. "This land and river have nurtured our family for three generations."

"But you promised..." Bernie pestered.

"Stop your bellyaching!" Anyone who observed Mom embracing Jeanne knew why we had to wait.

We hesitated before re-entering the river's surge. We knew we had witnessed an alarming scene. Next time we went swimming, I promised myself to watch out for Jeanne, my youngest sister. We were rooted in this river's ancient bed like Grandpa.

Bernie in the lead, Roger and Pat raced taking giant strides. We forced our legs through the swift, rushing water and searched for thick-bladed algae rugs to find our way back to our swimming hole.

I looked back at Mom and Jeanne, who clung to each other. Another earlier mother-daughter portrait flooded the reels of my mind. The picture of Mom rocking Karen, my baby sister who had fallen from a table and died three weeks later, remained indelible.

Cavorting voices and slicked bodies pushing upstream called me back. I listened to the river's song. The healing caress of the river's current distracted and calmed me.

An iridescent blue-green dragonfly alighted on my arm. I studied its delicate body and gauze-like wings, which undulated in the wind for a moment before it took flight. At that instant I realized I could crush it just like the river could have snuffed out Jeanne's life. How could this river, which provided so much therapeutic pleasure, hide within its powerful arms the destructive capability to drown my beloved sister?

Mom's authoritative voice called, "Take your last swim. It's time to go. Dad'll want supper soon." We scrambled one last time to paddle downstream and let the current carry our bodies closer to Mom and Jeanne on shore. A turquoise towel sheltered Jeanne from the cool breeze blowing through the trees. The cooling air hit our drenched bodies and made us shiver as we climbed out of the river. We welcomed a towel to dry off.

Church bells chimed the late afternoon hour. Its tolling was always a comfort to me, a security in our sometimes disordered life. Tomorrow school would come calling, and the arriving summer promised numerous river outings.

When we sat down to dinner that evening, Bernie baited like a gnat. "Remember, you said we could check out the river upstream?"

Without warning Roger blurted, "Dad, you should've been there. Jeanne fell into the river."

Mom was captured between Bernie's insistence and Roger's revelation.

I tensed. Would Dad forbid us to go now, guessing Jeanne almost drown?

"Sure took you long enough to get home. What's this about Jeanne?" Dad cut in, reaching for graham bread, his dark eyes sweeping our faces.

Mom placed a massive bowl of fried potatoes on the table. "Jeanne got caught in the river current," she explained, in an effort to salvage future river swims. "We learned how dangerous the river can be."

Dad was quick on the draw. "Could God be punishing you?"

How could he go there? My spirits drooped. I searched Mom's eyes, defiant and bright, and then panned by siblings' faces. We braced ourselves.

Mom stood, ready for battle. "God does not act like that!"

"How would you know?" Dad stated as he banged his fist on the table, jangling our plates, a signal the discussion was closed.

Mom made sense. We secretly cheered but did not dare look at each other. We had to prove Dad wrong the next time we swam the river. We ate in silence.

Dad rose from the table and on his way to the couch, he said, "No swimming until the potatoes are cultivated."

Bernie winced but said, "We'll work every day after school." His hope to adventure up river was still alive.

We looked at each other and pumped our heads up and down in silent agreement. We listened to the river's call like an incessant siren.

While climbing the steps to the girl's bedroom that night, the river spoke to me. The river offered us serenity, but held hidden peril while our family enjoyed rare unity of purpose amidst our usual agitation. Dad was the north bank, and Mom was the south bank. We lived this way between them, the only commonality being the rushing current lapped both shores.

X-RAYS

X-rays are good for looking through
the skin to see inside of you.

They show if bones are out of place
or if your molars need more space.

If someone swallows one thin dime,
x-rays reveal it every time.

They're useful, too, for finding where
a tumor may be lurking there.

They tell if disks are wearing thin
and let you know what shape you're in.

If bones are broken, not in line,
or if you have a crooked spine,

x-rays will let the doctor know
exactly where a cast should go.

X-rays bring cavities to light
and kidney stones. I think that's right,

but if you want to board a plane,
you may be x-rayed—how insane,

this tricky governmental twist—
to see if you're a terrorist.

—Grace Diane Jesson

PRESUMED INNOCENT
❧

Betty J. Vickers

Tommy Flowers had the smooth innocent face of a pre-pubescent
boy, but he turned forty-two the day Judge Walter Lucas ruled
Tommy not guilty of killing his employer, Gordy Boheen. Not
enough evidence to prove that Tommy blew Boheen's face off with
his own shotgun, even though Tommy had stumbled out of the
woods that day carrying Gordy's body like a rag baby doll. What
Judge Lucas didn't say—but everybody knew—was that even if
Tommy had done it, he was so mentally limited he likely wouldn't be
held responsible anyhow.

Most citizens of the town of Millersville said Judge Lucas had
dispensed justice exactly as they had elected him to do. Some were
not so sure. They said Judge Lucas was soft—that he should have
done his duty and sent Tommy to the chair even if he was a dummy.

"No doubt in my mind," declared Herb Tangborn, owner of
the General Mercantile. "Flowers done it. I don't care what Lucas
says, Flowers is guilty as sin. That's why he bolted soon as they
turned him loose. You'll never see old Tommy Flowers' face around
here again, no sir."

Cora, Herb's wife of four decades, disagreed. "Now you just hush up that kind of talk and keep your opinions to yourself, Herbert. Judge Lucas says Tommy is innocent, and that's good enough for me. Everybody knows Tommy loved the Boheens. He would never, in a million years, do anything to hurt Gordy or Vangie."

Tommy Flowers had walked onto the Rocking Horse Ranch one summer day six years earlier and asked Gordy Boheen for a job and a place to sleep. At first sight, Gordy had his doubts that the slight man dressed in bib overalls, tattered boots and a ratty straw hat was big and strong enough to handle the heavy work of running a ranch. But Gordy needed somebody, so he put Tommy to work cleaning out stables and doing odd jobs. It was a good decision. Tommy worked as hard as any man twice his size. Vangie spruced up a shed out back for him to bunk in. Although it was clear that Tommy had the IQ of a child, Gordy and Vangie treated him like he had as much sense as anyone else, and they paid him a decent wage.

To most of the townspeople, it hadn't made a lick of sense that Tommy had been arrested and tried for Gordy's murder. Folk said Sheriff Warren—no great shakes when it came to investigations of any type—had locked up Tommy so the town would think the Sheriff was doing his job. But several deeply suspicious citizens said Warren arrested the wrong one. They hinted, not too subtly, that the law ought to take a closer look at Vangie.

"I think she got tired of old Gordy's drinking and skirt-chasing and did him in herself," argued bald Jim Morehouse every chance he got while cutting hair over at the barber shop. Customers usually mumbled assent, whether they believed it or not, because Jim could turn cantankerous on a dime in the face of disagreement.

"Just look at how she sashshays around town in them tight jeans and sweaters," Jim fumed. "And all that piled up hair and them made-up eyes? Thinks she's better than any other woman in town, prancing around in them high-heeled, pointy-toed boots with her nose in the air."

Bucky Jarman, waiting his turn in the chair, laughed. "Being good-looking don't make her a murderer," he said. "Besides, I've seen your eyes on that sweater every time she walks by the shop. Maybe now that Gordy's out of the picture, you'll have a chance at the widow. 'Bout time you got married anyhow, ain't it?" Everybody guffawed except Jim.

"You watch your mouth, old man," Jim cautioned sourly. "You're next up in this chair and these new scissors just might slip."

The men laughed louder. The thought of old gutless Jim doing anybody any damage was too outlandish—as was the thought of the effeminate barber making advances to any woman, much less a fine specimen like Vangie Boheen.

Sheriff Warren had questioned Vangie—the next of kin is always suspect—but she had been up in Tallahassee visiting her mother in a nursing home at the time Gordy met his Maker. Running fingerprints on the trigger had been impossible. The gun had been caked with too much mud to lift any prints except a few of Gordy's.

Most of Millersville's population, however, favored a simpler and less frightening scenario. Several said Gordy had done himself in. Oh, not suicide—Gordy loved life too much for that. He had simply gone hunting that hot, August evening, tripped and fallen, and dropped his shotgun. It discharged into his face and killed him outright, they said.

A hunting accident was much more palatable than a murder by God-only-knew-who and for what purpose.

Still, the fact remained that if Tommy was innocent, then who did blow Gordy Boheen away? Was Vangie guilty in some way—and just lucky? Was it the irate, jealous husband of one of Gordy's many girlfriends, or some guy who had cheated at the cattle auction? Maybe even a *Deliverance*-type killing that had nothing to do with anything but somebody's downright rotten meanness. You never know for sure.

The furor over the judge's ruling quickly dwindled as several weeks went by and it became clear that Tommy had lit out for places unknown. People grew tired of the endless speculations about who was—or was not— probably guilty, and soon moved on to more current gossip.

Then, one morning just after sunup, Vangie saw Tommy dart out the door of his shack and head into the woods. She stepped out on the back porch and called his name several times, but Tommy was already out of sight and didn't answer.

Vangie subscribed to the hunting accident theory. She didn't believe Tommy would even know how to fire a shotgun and wouldn't have the guts to hurt a flea anyhow. Besides, now that Gordy was gone, she needed Tommy more than ever to help her with the ranch work. Plenty of men came around offering to help her, but Vangie knew what they were really after.

For the next three days, Vangie took fresh food out to the shack every day and, by the following morning, the food was gone. She watched from the kitchen window, hoping to see Tommy coming or going, but never caught even a glimpse. She wrote a note to him saying it was okay for him to stay, but tore it up when she remembered Tommy couldn't read. Finally, she settled for leaving a hand-drawn picture of a smiling face by his plate, hoping he would get the message.

On the fourth morning, she found a crudely penciled picture by his empty dishes. The drawing clearly depicted a stick figure Tommy walking down the road waving goodbye. *Damn!* she said under her breath. She craned her neck to look out the small window toward the county road in the distance, but could see nobody walking. There was no way to tell how long Tommy had been gone.

She knew he had a head start on her, any way you sliced it, but she was determined to try to find him anyway.

Vangie ran into the kitchen, grabbed her purse, and jumped into Gordy's black and red pickup parked by the back porch. When she reached the end of the long driveway, she stopped and hesitated. Then she turned right onto the county road, knowing Tommy would head away from town.

She drove as fast as she dared, all the while her eyes searching the terrain on both sides of the road. Nothing. After several miles, Vangie turned around and drove back toward Millersville, thinking perhaps Tommy had gone that way, after all, planning to skirt the town. She pulled into the Standard station at the edge of Millersville and stopped on the driveway with the motor running. It seemed clear that Tommy was gone. Further searching would be a waste of time.

Vangie swung out onto the blacktop and headed back toward the ranch. She slowed to make the turn into her driveway, but then drove past. She couldn't go home without making one last stab at finding Tommy. He had to be out there somewhere, but where? She drove until she saw the sign for the next town in the distance, then figured she may as well go home. Tommy was gone, and that was that.

She pulled to the side of the road and started to make a U-turn to head back toward Millersville. That's when she saw a man sitting on the ground by the city limits sign. The straw hat and baggy clothes were instantly familiar.

Quickly, she straightened the pickup and sped up the road toward him. It happened too fast for Tommy to run, but he was struggling to his feet when Vangie stopped in front of him. Wide-eyed, he snatched his straw hat from his head and held it over his chest.

"'Mornin', Miz Boheen," he stammered. "I was just goin' down the road gettin' out of town so as I won't bother you no more."

"Good morning, Tommy," Vangie said and smiled. "I've been looking all over for you. Come on and get in the truck."

"Oh, no, ma'am," he answered, hefting his loaded backpack and backing away. "I don't need no ride, thank ya, ma'am."

"Now, Tommy, I need you on the ranch and I know you need a job, so come on and get in." She reached over and opened the door.

Tommy hitched up the gallowses of his overalls and lowered his eyes. "But I figured you wouldn't want me to work for you no more—you know—after the jail and all."

Vangie smiled again at the shamefaced little man. "That's all in the past now, Tommy. The court found you not guilty, so you're a free man. Come on back and help me. I *want* you to work for me again."

Tommy turned his large blue eyes toward Vangie. "You do?" he asked. "You really want me to work for you—now after what—"

"Yes," she interrupted. "I want you back on the ranch. You're the best worker I've ever had. Get in, and let's go get some breakfast."

Tommy looked doubtful, but he shifted his load and climbed into the pickup. Vangie turned around in the road and headed back toward the Rocking Horse Ranch. Neither one spoke for the first mile. Tommy sat staring out the side window at the mottled brown range of mountains in the distance. Then he cleared his throat and turned to look at Vangie.

"Miz Boheen, seems like I ought to tell you—"

"No, Tommy," she cut in. "You don't need to tell me anything. Not now, not ever."

Tommy resumed gazing west toward the changing shadows on the mountains and the herds of cattle in the fields. He fidgeted with the clasp on his backpack and chewed a hangnail. When they neared the cattle guard crossing at the entrance to the ranch, he spoke again.

"But you don't know what happened out there—"

"No." Vangie held up her hand. "No, Tommy, I don't know what happened in the woods that morning, and I don't want to know. Just put it out of your mind. It's over and done with now, and we don't ever have to talk about it again. Understand?"

Vangie pulled the truck up to the back porch and turned off the engine. She was reaching for the door handle when Tommy spoke softly.

"Mister Gordy ought not to have been so mean to you like he was."

Vangie turned to look at Tommy, who was gazing down at the floor. He didn't look up as the seconds ticked by. She had no idea Tommy had ever been aware of Gordy's shabby behavior to her after his weekends of boozing and carousing. Had he heard Gordy yelling and cursing her for asking where he'd been? Worse yet, could Tommy have seen Gordy slap her and shove her off the back porch a few days before the hunting trip?

When a tear slipped down Tommy's face, Vangie was stunned. She sat with her hand on the keys and stared at him long moments before she finally spoke.

"You're right, Tommy. He ought not to have been so mean."

Then she reached over and patted Tommy's arm. "Let's go in and get some bacon and eggs before you start on that barn. We've got a lot of work to catch up with today."

A DREAM

Dad always wanted to see the walls
of Zion—walk in its gaunt winding halls
like a lion, revel in something rather new
than travel with horses Tom and Blue.
He wanted to walk in dust on Navajo stones
so different from the lost sheep's bones
or the call at mid-night of a calving cow;
He'd pull on a tight wool coat to plow
through snow and slide across an icy ditch
coming back with pride that no real glitch
kept him from helping with another baby calf.
Yes, years went by: Mother and he'd laugh
that soon they'd set a date to travel there.
But Fate baited them, took him on the lip of a prayer.

—Marilyn Ball

SOMEONE TO FOLLOW

Eric Bishop

The people in my group speak English, but the words confuse me. "Haystack" and "pillow" mean something different to Grand Canyon Boatmen than to someone raised in the dairy country of Northern Utah. I'd floated the San Juan River a year earlier, so I could row—sort of. But I'd never seen a rapid like this. I'm part of a private group on the biggest whitewater trip in North America, a float down the Colorado through Grand Canyon.

The chatter continues, and I elbow through to see what they're talking about.

Seventeen miles after launching at Lee's Ferry, the group is perched on a cliff, scouting Houserock Rapid. Twenty feet below, the Colorado River rumbles downstream, taking a sharp right turn. At the corner's apex, a boat swallowing hole churns next to a bus-sized boulder that's covered with cheese-grater-sharp ridges.

"A boat ripper," one man says.

At least I understand that part.

The men and some of the women point at the hole and the rock. Words like "current" and "wave" give me insight. My stomach heaves, as if the river is inside trying to burst free. I'm literally

45

moments away from rowing my raft, complete with eighteen days of gear and food around haystacks, tongues, and eddies, without knowing which is which.

"You can do this." My father's hand rests on my shoulder.

I swallow hard, refusing to puke the oatmeal and peaches I'd had for breakfast. A man named Roger approaches. Even through his mirrored aviator glasses, the stare makes me more aware of my inexperience. He looks away, shaking his head in disgust. For a second, his back turns and I think he'll leave. But then he spins around and steps forward. Beneath his hat-dana, the mirrored glasses reflect my image: pale, face drawn, mouth partially open. Several people flinch as a wave crashes below.

"Rapids do that," somebody explains. "They roar along, building to an explosion."

"You gettin' any of this?" Roger asks. I'm glad his eyes are hidden because his arms and elevated voice do plenty to convey disgust.

"Little bit." My voice cracks. "Kind of."

Roger sticks out among our group. He's floated The Colorado River through Grand Canyon thirteen times. He's been down Cataract Canyon close to fifty. Most importantly, Roger has never flipped his raft.

He turns to the river, stomps his sandals and scratches at his beard. Roger's annoyed, but he brings to mind a character from an old movie. He's Oddball, played by Donald Sutherland in "Kelly's Heroes," the hippie tank driver who saves Clint's ass.

"Do this," he says. "Put your boat three boat lengths behind mine." Roger shakes three skinny fingers in my face then pauses long enough for the rapid's roar to fill my head. "Do everything you see me do—and hope I don't fuck up!"

Middle-aged and lean, Roger, strides toward the beach.

Other boatmen, oars in hand, are ready to guide fully loaded rafts through the first serious rapid of the trip. Passengers unknot ropes from around rocks and tamarisk bushes, freeing the rafts into the calm water above the rapid.

"I think the captain has given us our orders." Dad's smile is obviously meant to man me up.

I nod and we walk toward the river. On the raft I notice as people in boats to the left and right buckle their life preservers and help one another cinch straps that had previously been loose. I blush, wondering if anyone noticed that I didn't remove my life preserver to scout the rapid. My father coils our bow-line, buckles up and launches us into the river.

The first raft plunges downstream ahead of Roger. For an instant, the boatman yanks then pushes the oars before his sixteen-foot raft disappears into the spray beyond the edge. Stroking forward, I estimate three boat lengths, but I oar too aggressively and fear that my bow will bump Roger's stern. As I back-paddle, the current accelerates Roger well beyond the distance I want.

"You heard him, Son," Dad yells over his shoulder from the bow, his voice barely discernable over the crashing water. "Do everything you see him do!"

In two oar strokes, Roger disappears, and then the current takes me. For the next fifteen seconds, I'm in the middle of an automatic carwash as water douches out my ear canals and peels back my eyelids. I work the oars and catch glimpses of Roger as I try to pinpoint where he is in the rapid so I can mimic his movements at the right times. On the downriver side of a hole a back-curling wave sends a wall of water over the bow and my father's head. It shows me how it looks from behind as water skier yells, "Hit it!"

Toward the bottom of the rapid, I angle my boat backwards, like Roger did. I pull away from the cheese-grater rock and hole that up close could easily swallow three rafts. The boat is

47

now full of water and I swear I'm rowing a tank instead of an inflatable.

"Rock over here!"

I yank on unresponsive oars that seem to be stuck in cement.

"An inch is as good as mile," Dad tells me as we slide past, barely missing.

"Thanks," I respond, rethinking how I tried my best to match Roger oar stroke for oar stroke.

I jump on the dry-box and pump my fists in the air. My victory dance is interrupted when I look down at Dad throwing water from the non-self-bailing raft. Across the swirling pool, Roger is helping his wife and son do the same.

Bear Bryant's words to his football players come to me.

"And when you get to the end-zone," the coach told them, "act like you've been there before."

I work the hand-held bilge pump to help return the rest of the water to the river.

"You guys okay?" Roger asks.

"Thanks to you—Captain."

"Wasn't pretty, but you made it." Then he gives me a "that'll do, pig" nod. "Let's get out of the eddy and run another one,"

That evening over steaks and Dutch-oven potatoes, we relive the adventure. Roger emerges my captain.

"Mind if I follow again?" I ask at the next big rapid.

"Catch me if I fall out." His polite response contrasts with my first impression and Houserock's f-bomb.

Grand Canyon lifts our eyes upward as the Colorado's current pushes us around each bend. The days roll together, and the June sun darkens our tan-lines. During stretches of flat water, I row close and pepper the Captain with questions about rafts, rivers, dry-boxes, and oars; he patiently answers them all.

At Tanner Rapid I go sideways through a hole. The river moves faster than my boat as I surf and nearly flip.

On day eight, we launch into adrenaline alley, a river section with rapids like Hance, Grapevine, and Sockdolager. The waves are bigger, the current faster. It exposes me for what I am: a hacking, clumsy rookie on the oars, slapping at surging water, while the Captain finesses through.

Each night we sleep under the stars, the river lulls us to sleep then becomes the soundtrack of our dreams. By day we savor new experiences with each bend. In addition to the rapids, we hike side canyons, visit ancient Hopi murals, shower under waterfalls, and watch the moon and sun rise above canyon walls.

By the time I learn the Captain works as a child psychotherapist at Primary Children's Hospital in Salt Lake City, my first impression of him is as far away as New York City.

"I bet the Captain's an amazing therapist," my father offers.

I think about how he coaches me through the rapids. How he tolerates my pestering questions, and picture him counseling grief-stricken children. Having two daughters under age five, I note everything he offers about raising kids.

The night before Grand Canyon's ugliest rapid, Lava Falls, I follow him through the chow line, taking identical portion sizes and placing my pork-chop and potatoes exactly where he does.

The Captain smiles.

The next morning, after studying his moves for close to two hundred miles, I know what the Captain will do. An unanticipated current spins his boat almost ninety degrees. I adjust beforehand to create a cleaner run than my mentor.

The second to last day of the trip, the Captain's somber mood makes me wonder if he's finally sick of having a tag-along.

Perhaps I'm a barnacle.

The final morning, I talk with others of the ice cream and fountain drinks we'll have at the first convenience store. The chatter continues at the takeout ramp as we unload the gear onto our waiting vehicles.

I twist the valves in my raft. The once-tight tubes deflate. A few yards downstream, the Captain, head bowed, stares at his raft's flaccid tubes like he's visiting a sick relative.

I want to trade all civilization's comforts for another day on the river.

Everyone hugs goodbye, except the Captain, who shakes hands. I'm surprised when he pulls me close.

"You've earned your wings."

"Thanks, Captain."

He moves across the parking lot and opens his SUV's door.

"Next time," he yells to me before climbing in. "I follow you."

TIME HOBBLES ON

They say I'm hard of hearing
    and I guess it must be true;
they sometimes have to tell me twice
    what they want me to do.

They say I don't see clearly,
    so they tell me not to drive
and I can't find my car keys.
    They want me to stay alive.

They say I need new dentures
    and my diet needs a boost—
not applesauce and yogurt
    and fruits that have been juiced.

They say I'm getting feeble,
    but I still can get around;
I'm not ready for a wheel chair
    since my walker's strong and sound.

They say I'm not a bother
    and they still laugh at my jokes,
but some time soon they'll move me
    to a home for older folks.

They say I am forgetful,
    but that's just a game I play,
for, secretly, I think my mind
    gets younger every day.

They think my days are numbered
    and my time is nearly gone,
but maybe I shall fool them all
    and just live on and on.

—Grace Diane Jesson

THE LAST MAN

Gabriel Taylor

Eighteen inches. A foot and a half of soil I have to remove before I can plant anything. A foot and a half of soil I can't touch with my skin. A foot and a half of dust and sand I can't breathe if I want to live. That's what the book says, the book I found down here with me. There really isn't much here besides a couple weeks worth of food and water, along with some batteries, a flashlight, first aid, and the book. I'm supposed to wait here until I have three days left of food and water, then run for it. I have to get away, get to the rendezvous point as quick as I can. The book says so. I hope I can remember which way is north from here. That's important, too. There's so much to remember, so many important things. If I forget one of them, do something wrong, I'm dead. Oh, God, watch over me.

How did it come to this? Sure, we were at war, sure, we had enemies, but didn't they know what would happen if they didn't stop the escalation? Did they think they could survive? Who knows, maybe they did survive. Lucky them. I shouldn't have survived. I only had a few seconds to get to the bunker before everything outside went to hell. I had no choice but to shut the doors. I waited inside, listening to the roar of the holocaust without. Lucky me.

It's warm down here and the air tastes stale. It's too early to go up, but I wonder. I've lasted so far. Three days, I think. There's supposed to be filters down here to keep the air breathable, but I can't find them. Maybe they're hidden to keep them protected. There are vents, but I don't feel any air moving. If I get too tired and feel like I'm going to pass out, I'll have to go up. The book says if anything goes wrong with the filters, I'll have five days of air down here if I stay calm and limit movement. Less if I'm nervous and fidgety. I may have to move tomorrow. Can't stop my hands from shaking.

Potassium iodide pills. They look like horse pills. As big as quarters almost. I hate pills. Oh well. I can't stay down here another day. I'm getting cooked. And the air is going bad. I found an O2 meter behind the first aid kit. That's why I have to take the potassium pills. The air above may still be full of dust. I'll have my face mask, but I'm bound to get some of it in my lungs. Hopefully, the pills will block it from getting into my lymph nodes, or whatever. I don't understand how any of this works, I'm just following what the book says. I'll leave tonight. Everyone dies sooner or later. I wonder if dying down here is really any worse than out there.

I made it, so far. It took me over two days but I made it. The radiation counter sang when I stuck my head up, but now it only beeps occasionally. Everything itches but the book says not to give in. I can't spare any water for a bath, either, so I have to live with it. I have a couple more days worth of food and water. I'll need to find more.

The book said there were some other bunkers near here. I hoped to find people here. There's no one, and the bunkers weren't sealed before the blast so the supplies are ruined. The sky is dark nearly all the time and thunder storms constantly loom on the horizon. The lightning scares me. I've never seen anything so powerful. Lights up the entire horizon. Nothing looks familiar now. There are mountains and valleys everywhere, and they use to be plains. If the storms come too much closer I'll have to move again. Rain doesn't help anything grow now; it only kills.

I moved on two days ago and found a bunker today. The doors were shut but not locked. No one inside. I have more supplies now.

Been here a few days. The storms are still on the horizon. I stay down in the bunker most of the time, waiting. The book says the nearest rendezvous point is a little further north from here. As far as I can remember, there aren't any more cities between here and there, just small towns. No shelters, fewer supplies, and to go north means getting closer to the storms.

Deep down I think we all knew it would come to this. We just didn't know when it would come. There wasn't any warning. On my way to work, alarms started going off and I was next to the bunker. In the beginning I wondered if it would come by accident. Now I see things clearly, the way people were. Someone wanted this to happen. In war, lots of people pull the trigger but only a few have blood on their hands.

I think I'm dying. Part of me wants to. Blisters cover most of my body. Even with all the pain I managed to run when the storms came. I've never seen a sky change so fast. The dark clouds thrashed around as the lightning shrieked down everywhere. There were still a few buildings standing nearby. They're not there anymore, but I survived. The rain was cold even though it felt like it was boiling. I ran north through it all. The storms came from the north, so I might have shaved off a few minutes or maybe even an hour from the time I had to spend in the storm. I might have shaved more than that off my own life. I took more potassium. It may help.

I found them today. The others. They're all dead. The air filters in their bunker must not have worked, either. There were so many of them down there. Their air must have run out after a couple hours. I don't have the strength to bury them. I guess a bunker's as good as anything now. There's another rendezvous point to the east of here, then one more north of that. I have to keep moving. The rain makes my radiation counter sing. I think I'm bleeding inside.

The last couple of days I haven't been able to eat. I've been throwing up constantly and there's blood mixed in the bile. I managed some water today, but I have to ration it. I can't waste what I have. It isn't much. The sores on my arms and legs have begun to heal, at least. I keep taking the potassium pills. I feel better when I do, but that may just be a placebo. My radiation counter still chirps regularly. There's only a couple miles before the next rendezvous point. I travel as far as I can each day. It may take me a while.

Well, I'm still alive. That's something at least. The batteries in my radiation counter are dying. I can only turn it on once in a while to check if I'm safe. The storms seem to be calming down. I feel a lot better, too. I'm not so shaky as I was before. I've made it to the second rendezvous point. Same problem as the others. At least I'm not running out of supplies for now.

I don't know why I'm writing this. I've been wondering about it the last couple of days. I don't know what got me started, but now I don't know if I can stop. Not until I either find the others or I die. I don't care which it is. I don't want to live like this. It may be childish, but I can't bare this solitude. I don't speak aloud anymore because I'm afraid I won't stop talking to myself. My family lived near the last rendezvous point. Maybe they're still alive. Perhaps it's foolish of me to get my hopes up. I do hope.

Why do we believe so easily the lies we tell ourselves? We said we'd win, that ours was the greater cause. I'm sure every side in a war says such things. Maybe no one lied. We all saw things from a different perspective. Conditional morality, I guess. Who knows, maybe we were wrong and they were right the whole time. Traditionally, the winners write history and that dictates the right or wrong of the war. Maybe no one won this time; no one was right.

I was married, once. That doesn't matter now, I know, but I thought I should write it down. We never had any children. I regret that now.

I'm half a mile from the rendezvous point, I think. Smoke rises from that direction. Tomorrow I should reach them, if my strength holds out. Ever since the rain I've been so tired and weak. I didn't want to admit it. A couple hours of walking is all I've been able to manage the last few days. I'm too exhausted to do much more. Hopefully that rising smoke is from camp fires. The book says this shelter could house hundreds of refugees and even has a medical facility. Maybe I'll finally find the others, find my family. Maybe I'll be dead before I get there.

Thought I'd take a rest before I climb this last hill. I should be able to see the rendezvous point from the top. If they're not there, then I'll know that this must be my penance, my hell, to wander through this dead world. Or maybe they're alive and I can still be redeemed for what part I played in all this. So tired. I'll take a nap and then climb the last hill.

LENA

(a excerpt from the book, *For Cryin' Out Loud!*)

❦

Dianne Hardy

Even for the 1950s, Mama and Daddy were prejudiced; most people
in the Uintah Basin were. They were loud about it, too. I remember a
man in our ward confidently bearing his testimony from his
preeminent position, "After that night I didn't give them young fellas
any more whiskey—quit drinking entirely—wasn't gonna be like an
Indian anymore." Ward members nodded in agreement, pleased at
the change in the guy.

   The people of Roosevelt and Vernal hated the Ute Indians
that lived on a reservation separating the two towns. When I was
five, Mama read from a book about the different tribes that the Utes
were the most uncivilized, eating the family dog rather than hunting
for food. I looked at Bubbles, the tiny brown and black Mexican
Chihuahua on my lap, and I hated them, too.

   Uintah County, encompassing the Ute reservation, built an
elementary and junior high school on the west end of the reservation,
but close to Roosevelt, which sat directly across the county line.
Although public schools, they serviced all students in the area, Indian
or white. Roosevelt's Union High School was built to straddle the

Duchesne and Uintah County lines. It was financed by both districts and accommodated the students on the west side of Uintah County, plus the students of Duchesne County. The people of Uintah County found it an effective way to "keep the Indians on their own side" and out of the Vernal schools.

Only occasionally did Indians live directly in the Roosevelt Township, so Daddy, as principal of the elementary school, hardly had to deal with them. He made certain none were in my classes, and I never knew an Indian until I entered junior high school, where there were a handful. The numbers increased somewhat when the Mormon Church implemented the Indian Placement Program in 1954.

The placement program was designed to offer improved educational and economic opportunities to Indian students, who were church members of at least ten years of age. In addition to proselytizing, Mormon missionaries were used to recruit qualifying families, those who lived long distances from schools or those who didn't have the economic means to meet their child's needs.

The program was only minimally successful in the basin because of the conflict between the church's stance and a member's racial bias. Many people said nothing, just didn't get involved, and some openly said things like, "We've got our own Indians and we damn sure don't need any more."

It was a commonly held idea that Indians would never become educated; they simply couldn't learn. Mama and Daddy were highly critical of the program.

"An Indian's an Indian, no matter which tribe claims him. Indians mixing with our kids can only mean trouble," Daddy ranted. "Pretty soon he'll want to date white girls and who knows what will happen then!"

In August we kids anxiously awaited UBIC, the Uintah Basin Industrial Convention, a three-day celebration full of all kinds of events. My favorite was the art show, which I entered each year. There were also shows for babies, pets, talent, flowers, and vegetables. Eating contests were big; there was one for watermelon and one for pie.

Donald, a kid my age, usually won the pie-eating event. When he was in the seventh grade, he ate six whole pies, while grown men ate three or four. Now, a year later he was even fatter, so he could probably down seven or eight.

The last event was a Saturday night dance on the tennis court with Wardle's Orchestra. It lasted until 11:30, when fireworks went off, signaling the end of UBIC until the next year.

I got up late Saturday morning because I'd been to the movie in the park Friday night. I hurriedly bathed Bubbles, drying her until her dark coat shone like Daddy's Sunday shoes. I fastened the leash to her collar, strung a red ribbon around her neck, and headed for the pet show. When the judges asked what she could do, I told them she liked to chew bubble gum, and that was how she got her name. I guess they weren't impressed because she didn't win, but I didn't care because she was my dog and the best of the bunch.

As I was leaving for home, I spotted Lena, a student I casually knew from junior high. She shyly approached and asked if she could walk home with me and use our telephone to call her placement mother to come get her. She said she wanted ample time to get ready for the evening dance.

Lena, a Navaho Indian, was beautiful—tall and slender with waist-long shiny black hair and intelligent black eyes. She was so beautiful and gracious I couldn't help staring at her. Once Daddy quipped, "If you were a man, you'd have the shit beat out of you, the way you stare at people, Dianne."

Lena's family had a German shepherd named Andy, so we talked about our dogs, interests, and hobbies. She loved to do bead work and draw scenery from around her home in Shiprock, New

Mexico. I told her about the charcoal drawing I entered in the art show, a picture of my two younger sisters playing by a playhouse Daddy made for them. We stopped by the art exhibit and excitedly saw that my entry won a blue ribbon and was selected for the state fair.

Lena and I decided to walk home slowly in order to get to know one another better. I told her I played the piano and she said she played a native flute. We made plans to get together and work on a couple of pieces for the school talent assembly in October.

"I'm so happy," she said, grabbing my hand. "I didn't make many friends last year. Now I'll be starting ninth grade with my best friend. I've been awfully homesick and unable to do some of the Indian things I like, but now I think taking part in the placement program was maybe a good decision."

"We will be best friends, Lena," I assured her. "Let's be sure to register for our classes together, especially art class. Maybe we can collaborate on some projects."

All too soon we were home. While Lena called her placement mother, I hurriedly picked up my bedroom so I could show her my things. She began browsing through the book shelves.

"I've never seen so many books," she said, "except in a library. I like to read and am getting better at it, but I don't know any of these books."

I looked for one she'd enjoy; then I ran onto *Gone With the Wind*.

"You'll surely like this one, Lena. It's a great love story, and you may borrow it."

She smiled and thanked me. "I've never seen one this thick, but I promise I'll read it—every word, Dianne."

Next I showed her some family pictures of our vacations to Yellowstone National Park and Liberty Park in Salt Lake City. Mama was in her bedroom reading, which meant I didn't have to introduce Lena or explain her presence. Daddy was working, as usual.

But five minutes later I heard his car barreling up the street. Then he was coming in the front door.

Oh no! What will I do? I can't get her out. He's always working; why does he have to come home now? Please, Heavenly Father, don't let him hear us.

As I frantically searched for a reason to have Lena whisper, she saw a family picture and broke into peals of laughter. "You look like you're posing for the camera, Dianne."

It was true. My childhood pictures all looked staged as I held in my stomach in order to look thinner—a problem Lena would never have. The shame of wanting to eat—no, loving to eat—had been with me forever.

I froze, heart pounding, as Daddy came down the hall. Maybe he'd go to Mama's bedroom—but no, he heard Lena laughing. Without knocking he opened the door and stared wide-eyed, his face flushing bright red with anger. Veins in his neck stood out as he clenched and unclenched his fists.

"Daddy, this is Lena," I stammered, my mouth dry.

She stretched out her hand in greeting. He ignored her, glared at me, and sputtered, "Get that Goddamn Indian out of here—now!"

I have a hard time remembering what happened next. Time stopped. I believe Lena set *Gone With the Wind* down on my bed and started walking toward the front door. I followed her out on the lawn to wait for her ride. She wouldn't look at me and neither of us spoke. It was just minutes before Sister Swenson came, but it seemed like an eternity. As Lena got into the car, I saw she was crying.

That night there was a talent show before the dance. I didn't go to either, yet I was at the park well before time. I spotted Marie, a wild girl from my school. She was smoking with a group of Indian boys from the west side school. I said hello to her and abruptly turned to one of the boys, a stranger to me.

65

"I'm sixteen—and ready for fun."

He gave me a questioning look and without a word, I led him across the street to my church.

That night I let him do things I'd never thought of.

I hate you, Daddy, and you too, God. I'll give you Indian! Look at me, at what I'm doing beneath your church window.

DEEPENING TRIALS

(a excerpt from the book, *Tales of Valor*)

Irene Hastings

It's the screaming—the awful screaming. I have to hide. Meribel curled herself into a small ball on the ground behind the wood box near the shed. She felt more like a small child than a nearly grown woman of sixteen.

"Stay put and don't come out no matter what you see or hear," Ma said, hiding her.

"I can't stand the screaming—is it Ma? Sissy?—Granny Mae? Why is this happening—are we being punished?"

Meribel pressed her hands over her ears, trying to shut out the noise. Her body shook so hard she thought the mob would hear. The flannel gown Ma made her was little help from the winter's cold.

Help us, God. Don't let my family be hurt.

The sky was orange with flames from burning homes. The desperate cries of children, calling for their mamas, their papas, were a rapier through her heart.

Please don't let them find me. God, help us—me and Ma and Pa and Sissy and Granny Mae and Billy.

69

The awful stink of burning wood, hot tar, blood that smelled like rusty nails, filled the air like a noxious cloud. Meribel eased her cramped limbs a bit in each direction, trying not to be seen from her hiding place, remembering her promise to Ma. She sneaked a look around its side and wished she hadn't. Women and children ran in haphazard directions, trying to escape rifles, whips, and knives of a mob gone berserk. Menfolk in the camp fought back with anything at hand: pitchforks, pieces of wood, even rocks. Women screamed and fought with strength dredged up from fear. But they were outnumbered.

Smoke curled from their cabin across the clearing. Everything disappeared, vanished in the demon's molten breath. Soon there was nothing left but a smoldering pile of rubble. The metal handle of Ma's new water pump stuck up as if to say, "It didn't get me!"

Meribel squeezed her eyes shut, whimpered like a lost animal. Numbness and fatigue claimed her as she imagined Pa's arms around her, saying, "It's all right" baby, it's all right."

Time passed without meaning. Huddled into a little ball, Meribel felt nothing. Not the cramped muscles, freezing cold, terror. Nothing. The flames burned down, leaving little more than ashes and smoke with bits and pieces of intact possessions. Screams subsided. The mob did its work, accomplished its purpose and left, leaving a terrible legacy of death, destruction, broken lives. But not broken spirits, not all.

As the first light of dawn broke, people shuffled around, trying to find family, friends, some part of their lives, feared lost.

"Maribel, Meribel, where are you?" *Father's voice?* "Meribel, answer me!" She looked up at Pa as he moved the wood box, finding her crouched against it. His shaggy beard and work-roughened hands never felt so good as he folded her into his arms with the biggest bear hug she'd ever had.

"Pa! Oh, Pa, you came. You came."

"My sweet girl, you knew I would, didn't you?" Tears flowed.

"I was so scared, Pa, I thought you were dead and they'd find me."

"I know, baby, I know. But Pa's here now. It's all right." He kissed her forehead and wiped her tears with the back of his grimy hand, leaving smudges of smoke on her fair skin.

"Don't cry, Meri. The tears in your big blue eyes make my heart feel like it's going to break." She gulped big sobs back in her throat.

"Where's Ma and Sissy and Granny Mae?" Pa didn't answer.

Pa helped Meribel to stand up on shaky legs as she looked around. It was like the end of the world—Sodom and Gomorrah in Pa's bible after God destroyed them. Women gathered up their family members, one by one, like lost sheep. Meribel heard quiet sounds of sobbing, gasps of recognition for a son or daughter lying helpless on the ground. Sharp screams pierced the air when one was found with open eyes that would see no more. Tears scored sooty paths down cheeks as families were gathered. Some dead, some wounded, some alive. Others hid in a nearby grove of trees, where night was their friend, afraid to come out.

Pa placed his hand on Meribel's arm. "Meribel, well, Ma—Ma got hurt real bad. She's calling for you."

"Oh, no Pa!" Meribel's hand covered her mouth in horror.

"Shh—I've got to say this now," said Pa. "Sissy's a wonder for such a small fry. She hid up in the branches of yonder tree—Billy got hit by bullet—it just clipped the side of his head—nothin' to get upset over."

"Oh, Pa!"

"Be strong, Meribel. Your ma needs you—come on, be my brave girl."

"But, Granny Mae? Where's Granny Mae, Pa?"

"Her heart just gave out, Meri. She's gone to Jesus."

71

Meribel hid her face in her hands an sobbed. Pa stood helpless; he wanted to make everything better, but could only hold Meribel close to his chest and pat her back, like he did when she was a baby.

"Don't cry, baby. It's over now. It's what Granny Mae would want. 'Sides, your dark curly hair and those blue eyes will always be a reminder of Granny Mae." He fluffed her hair with one hand.

No. I don't think Granny Mae would want to leave us. 'Specially now. All those plans we made for her seventy-ninth birthday. She had a quilt frame ready—she loved sitting on the front porch swing, watching the stars at night. No, no, no—she wouldn't want to leave us.

"Yes, Papa, guess so." Meribel looked away.

Jackson, Missouri, was a peaceful, industrious city, a place of refuge for the beleaguered Mormons, until the mobs came. Meribel was only six years old when the "saints" were driven from their homes in Kirtland, Ohio. They'd left after dark, driving over bumpy dirt roads like the hounds of Hades were after them.

Now it was happening all over again, only worse. As Meribel stumbled through the rubble and devastation alongside Pa, she thought of her best friend, Lucy, walking home from school with her just a few days ago. Lucy seemed quiet and didn't say much.

"What's wrong, Lucy? You mad at me or something?"

Lucy reached out her hand to Meribel. "Meri—I just gotta say this and get it out. My pa told me I can't see you anymore. I feel real bad, but he said if he caught me with you, he'd wear out a green willow on me." Lucy's eyes filled with tears and she looked down at the dirt path.

"But, Lucy, whatever for? Did I do something wrong? Why's your Pa so mad at me?

"Well—everybody hereabouts says you're one of those 'Holy Joes,' and you don't belong with our kind of folks." She let go of

Meribel's hand. "I'm awful sorry, Meri." Lucy turned and ran for home without looking back.

Meribel stood still and straight as the fence posts lining the road, watching her friend as he disappeared from sight, trying to make sense of it all. She thought of how some of the kids at school poked fun at Mormon kids.

"Why don't ya go back where ya came from. We don't want ya here."

"Yeah, 'fore we know it, the whole town'll be crawlin' with your kind, a'stirrin' up decent folk with your strange ideas."

Elias, in her school class, picked up a rock and threw it at Meribel, but she ducked just in time. Even grow-ups looked at her strange-like. *Why do they hate us so much?*

Now here they were, driven out again, their homes burned to ashes by folks they knew, turned into hate-filled mobs. Meribel pulled her nightgown tighter around her, looked at the scorched earth and felt the bitter bite of morning air.

I thought this would be a better place. A peaceful place where we could just be happy like everyone else. Thought it'd be different this time. Meribel remembered their comfortable homes, their school with a bell on top, the church at the center of town where they gathered, prayed, sang their hymns without being afraid.

"Hurry, girl, hurry. Your ma and the kids need us. Don't stand there daydreaming." Pa grabbed her hand to hurry her along.

Meribel paused, looked at her father. "Pa—where's Brother Joseph? Did they kill him?"

Joseph Smith, known as their prophet, was loved by all. Young, strong, good-looking, sun-streaked hair, penetrating blue eyes. He played kick-the-ball with the kids, wrestled with the older boys. Joseph stopped by saints' homes to see how everyone was doing, maybe have dinner with them. Almost every day, Meribel saw him walk the streets, help dig foundations, saw lumber for new homes.

"Brother Joseph's gone over to Zion's Camp to get help for us," Pa said, knowing it would be too late to save them from the mobs or keep their homes from burning. Zion's camp was about 200 miles away and time had run out.

Ma was in the shed behind a house that had escaped the fire. Her thin body was lying on a pile of straw, covered over with some makeshift flannel that a neighbor brought. Her eyes were closed. Sissy sat by her side, crying.

She's awful quiet. Too quiet. "Pa?"

"Your Ma's in a bad way." Pa's voice sounded wooden, tight. "Try not to upset her."

Meribel took her mother's hand in hers. It was limp, like Sissy's rag doll. She felt the blister on the palms of Ma's hand where she hoed beans and corn. It was floppy, disconnected from her arm, not like Ma's strong hand.

"Ma, it's me, Meri, I'm here."

Her mother raised he dark-rimmed eyelids, like they weighed a ton. "Meri, my Meri—are you all right, child?"

"Yes, Ma, I'm fine. I hid like I promised you." Meri tried to swallow the lump in her throat, big as a watermelon.

"Good child—always obedient." The words died in Ma's mother. Her eyes shut again.

"She's alive—just." Sister Allen, the neighbor lady, tut-tutted and wrung her hands helplessly, not knowing what to do amid all the chaos. Instinctively, she gathered the children in her arms, clucking like a mother hen. "Shh, shh. It's all right, it's all right."

But it wasn't, and they knew it.

After ministering to the sick, injured and dying, the saints met in the town square, one of the few remaining sites of their once-proud town.

Sidney Rigdon, one of town's religious leaders, stood before them, spoke with solemnity, his voice breaking with emotion. "Brothers and Sisters, I fear the wrath of the mob is not yet finished, not as long as one of us lives, as long as we stand on one square foot of Jackson County soil." Wails and moans came from the crowed.

"We'll fight 'em to the death! I'll give 'em a taste of my rifle," one loud voice proclaimed.

"No, Brother Morton, that is not God's way. These trials and persecutions are sent to temper us as Isaiah prophesied, in the caldron of fire." He paused, saddened, helpless at the despair inscribed upon their faces.

"More like the fires of Hell," someone mumbled, "and we're *sure* getting burned."

"But we will prevail." Brother Rigdon shook his fist at the smoke-filled air. "We will prevail, I tell you. We'll stay firm in the belief that God will show us the path. I promise you, angels will go before us in the wilderness."

"Where will we go, Sidney? What does God want us to do?" Meribel's Pa, Josiah, asked the question they all needed answered.

"We'll leave this accursed place today—cross the Missouri River, put it all behind us, find refuge in Illinois." He stopped, looked past their faces at a place only he saw.

"There, we'll gather our strength, make our future plans."

"How're we goin' to cross that mean old river in the middle of November?" shouted James Rasmussen, over the heads of his four children, in a pathetic huddle. "Yes," he continued, "and if we do make it to the other side, will they let us stay there?"

"Brother Joseph will muster the brethren at Zion's Camp and bring relief to us," Brother Waldron said, with a positive nod of the head. Others were not as optimistic, speaking in low tones among themselves.

75

"Hope he makes it soon, or we're done fer," muttered aged Hepiziah Brown, her bent frame leaning on her cane, the cane she wielded with ferocity before being knocked to the ground by one of the mob. "I'm getting too old fer this nonsense!"

"We'll salvage what we can," said Brother Rigdon. "Food supplies will be loaded in one of the good wagons, hidden in the grove of trees. We'll leave soon as darkness falls."

At dusk they gathered at the town square. A prayer was offered. There was nothing left for then to do but move on. One by one, two by two, families headed for the roaring Missouri River banks, with Sidney Rigdon going before them, like Moses leading the Israelites out of bondage.

Each step of the way they looked over their shoulders, fearful that remnants of the mob would strike again. They dared not talk nor sing. Meribel's mother was placed in a rickety cart belonging to the Fife family. Billy, tall for his fourteen years, wore a soiled rag around the wound on his head, a badge of new manhood. He trudged along in the moonless night beside Meribel and Sissy. Lanterns lit the way over the treacherous, frozen ground; they looked like an invasion of fireflies.

"Pa, can't we stop and build a fire? My feet are frozen." Sissy was still wearing her "everyday" shoes without socks, hastily pulled on as she ran to hide from the mob.

"No, Sis. I wish we could, but we've got to hurry afore any of the mob find out we've left—or where we're headed." *Even if we knew.* Pa tried to hide his despair from the children. Like others, the clothes on his back were all he had.

Meribel stumbled along in the dark, walking close by her mother's side. *Ma looks poorly. If only she had her winter blanket to keep her warm.* Friends had given what little they could spare to those in need. Someone had tucked a hand-knit afghan around Ma's thin body. Still, she shivered.

On they went, not knowing how they would cross the river nor what awaited them on the other side. Where would they find food, shelter from the biting November wind, the flakes of snow beginning to swirl around them? Although driven by fear and the need to survive, they clung, in varying degrees of faith, to God's plan for them.

It was a pitiful band of pilgrims who struggled with all their remaining strength to reach the river's bank. The wind howled in unholy pain. Snow covered their forms until they resembled spirits.

Meribel looked at the story sky above, at the raging waters ahead.

Only the angels can save us now.

HOME IS THE SOLDIER, HOME FROM THE WAR

Beth Shumway Moore

During World War II a yellow telegram terrified the recipients because it was the method of informing families that their loved one had been wounded or killed. No details then, just the stark "we regret to inform you that your son/daughter/father was wounded/dead on ---." With the arrival of modern technology, I wonder what method is used to notify families today?

It wasn't the news of the death of my brother, Hyrum Smith Shumway, when our family received their yellow telegram shortly after D Day in World War II. Its message was terse, and only told us he was wounded. He had survived the invasion of France on Omaha Beach, then tragically, only a few months later a land mine exploded, leaving him blind and seriously injured. As soon as he was able to travel, the army moved him to Dibble General Army Hospital in Menlo Park, California. My mother and I went to see him immediately. Our shock and heartbreak can only be understood by others who have suffered similar news.

When we first saw him, my brave little mother reached to hug her tall son, while I wanted to keep walking. This man with the white cane, hesitant walk, and scarred face couldn't be my brother. I didn't want to face the horrible reality of what had happened to him, but there wasn't any choice. It helped when the doctors, nurses, and all who worked with him told us of his immediate and courageous acceptance of his fate, and how he helped give the other wounded boys the courage to do the same. As Director of the Blind for the state of Wyoming, he spent his time not only improving the lives of the blind, but also touching countless people with his courage and optimism. His glass wasn't even half full. It was filled to the brim.

When I heard the news of my brother's death at 89, coming 67 years after our yellow telegram, I cried and cried, but it wasn't because of sorrow. Oh no, while the tears ran down my cheeks, I was filled with joy that bubbled inside me. Joy that he was free from pain at last. My first thought was, *he can see.* He can see the many loved ones waiting for him, and the happiness that has to be surrounding him is beyond our human comprehension.

My children and I immediately went to Cheyenne to join a large number of family members gathered in what his children called "A Celebration of a Life and Farewell to a Great Man." Considering the life he'd lived it was a much more apt description than the dreary word "funeral."

During his life, Smith (as we called him) took his family to Aspen Grove, a vacation spot near Provo, Utah, area several times through the years. It was a loved getaway for President Monson, who visited with Smith often, then later honored him twice in The Church of Jesus Christ of Latter-day Saints annual conference. Shortly before Smith died, President Monson sent a personal letter, stating he considered Smith among the greatest men he'd ever known. This recognition from the man he revered as a Prophet had a special place for Smith, even though it was one of the many, many awards he won for his accomplishments. His awards were climaxed with being knighted Sir Hyrum Smith Shumway in France on the 60th anniversary of D-day on June 5, 2004, a grateful tribute by a country who honored his sacrifice.

Memories darted in and out of my mind as I mingled and visited, proclaiming how happy I was that he could see again. Memories of a six-year-old brother who, so the story goes, bragged to everyone on the day I was born that now he had a sister. How he woke me when I was around three years old, so pleased to give me a tiny iron table and chair set he'd saved his pennies to buy. How he pinched my throat once when he zipped up my snow suit, and he cried more than I did. Even though I don't remember, I'm sure he helped with my first steps when I learned to walk because later he taught me how to jump rope, to count, to ride a bike, and to dance. As I remember, he was the only one who listened to me when I began to read. He was overjoyed that I shared his love of reading and books. Years later, in the long winter evenings when our family sat reading, Smith was always nibbling on apples, and our brother, Charley, would tell him to "quit smacking." Smith was such a tease that he smacked even harder.

I remember him debating, with himself, as to whether he could really afford the three dollars for a book that was advertised on the radio. It was a condensation of the greatest books ever written. He decided he had to have it. I still remember when it came. It was an exciting day. Books were so scarce and treasured back then. No place in our little Wyoming town sold books, and our county library was very limited. We were lucky that Mom had inherited her father's library and we had many books compared to most people. That situation must be hard to relate to in today's technological world when not only books were scarce, but all we had was a radio with poor reception because of the mountains surrounding our valley.

The thought of how Smith could never read a book again has always tormented me. But now he can! We must continue reading in heaven. Yet because of technology and his ever-present tape recorder, he was probably one of the best read people I ever knew.

Images came to my mind of how Smith ran everywhere. He milked cows morning and night at the edge of town. His friend, Jodi Fillerup's father, ran the local dairy. Smith would run there and home every morning and night. There weren't many cars in those days, and we were one of the rare families who owned one. We'd have our last drive in the autumn, Dad would put the car in the garage for the winter, and we'd look forward to our spring drive, especially after Smith got his driver's license. For the most part, people walked, or ran, if they wanted to go anywhere.

Smith had such a good build, broad shoulders, narrow hips, erect carriage, and a strong, forceful walk. When he lost his sight and was forced to depend on someone else or his cane, he no longer had the freedom and spring of his normal walk and run.

Smith was a track star at the University of Wyoming, and he'd ride the bus home for college break, passing our house that was two miles from town, then get off in town and run back home. I remember watching for him, after hearing the bus go by when we were expecting him. He'd come running down the road, his hair blowing in the wind, and his face alight with his love of life.

Smith lived and acted a life in which blindness had no part. He portrayed that it was so insignificant that I heard different people say many times, "I forgot he was blind." Blindness wasn't going to beat him, no way. He vowed he would beat being blind and he did. Never did blindness keep him from achieving any goal he set himself, or if it did, no one ever knew. A few of us might have guessed, but we never knew for sure.

His eight children motivated him to become a magician. He always worried his children might feel a loss, or that they'd missed something, by having a blind father. I'd scold him severely because "all children should have such a Father as he was."

82

As a magician Smith could go to their schools and entertain their friends. He became very accomplished, not only entertaining his family, but he performed many places. He amazed audiences with his skill. Smith became a member of the National Magician's Society, and continually learned new tricks to add to his presentations. He was offered a lucrative deal to tour the country as *The Blind Magician,* but he refused the offer. That wasn't why he'd honed his skills. Yet he performed freely in public wherever he was invited. To give happiness and joy to others was always his goal in everything Smith did.

He also did this by using his talents of playing the violin and the harmonica. Not satisfied with playing his harmonica for public audiences, he'd often go for a *walk around the block* in the evening with one or more of his children. Many times I'd see other children, and even adults, follow after him as if he'd been the Pied Piper his harmonica weaved its spell. After he retired, he organized three bands, one of which he called a "Kitchen Band." The name came because they were senior citizens who, if they didn't have an instrument, could make their own, such as a wash board, a pan to beat on with a spoon, or a triangle with nails. Smith's Kitchen Band had an accomplished pianist who made their music sound surprisingly good. These bands volunteered at hospitals, rest homes, and anywhere else they were invited. Smith found great joy in the happiness he spread and, most important, the wordless message he sent of how he'd survived his disabilities.

Yet as I tried to express how I was so happy, I could hardly contain myself when I thought of him seeing again, I didn't feel anyone really understood. After returning home and reliving the wonderful memories and talks with so many family members, I remembered and puzzled over why I hadn't felt that same joy from anyone else. Then it hit me! I understood.

Everyone there but his dear childhood friend, Merrill Asay, and I, only knew a blind Smith. There was no memory of a father, grandfather, great-grandfather, uncle, cousin, friend, bishop, patriarch, etc., who could see. It was impossible to relate and understand my joy when I kept saying, "Smith can see again," over and over. Their joy was as great, only different.

But Merrill's tears and mine were a lot the same, I'm sure— the memories of a loved man who could see again at last. And yes, daughter Elizabeth, in your wonderful talk, when you said you wondered if your mother would know your father in his restored body, yes, yes she will. And feel more joy than anyone when the young man she fell in love with, can see her again. He will be able to see his loved daughter, Joan, who went before him, for the first time too.

Yet another memory has to be told of when a friend of his made the comment, "How sad it is that Smith can't see his children." I remember saying, "Oh yes he can. I followed him around more than one night when he would listen to each of his eight children say their prayers. As they prayed he would lightly run his fingers over their faces. Oh yes, I always believed he knew what they looked like, in a special way, maybe it was their souls he saw through his sensitive fingers."

His trials are over, and I firmly believe a loving Heavenly Father welcomed him with the words, "Well done, thou good and faithful servant," and many more wonderful words that Smith can tell us about some day.

Are you crying yet? I am!

PAINTING, UNTITLED

Give me the words to paint with: umber, and sienna;
prepare a blank space, sharpen me a dark, pine wood brush;
let me with deliberate strokes sketch a lifetime.
Fill the space with cerulean sky, dun grass, and far distances.
Then with gentle hand, render the fine details of smiles,
embraces, your warm naked back, the scent of your hair.

With broad blotter and palette knife, let me recreate a childhood,
one with fathers and open summers without stares. In strokes of
vermillion be fearless, for I will chase away all doubts.
Let me paint over the crosshatched grays with deep cobalt,
which salves your skin from the harsh tawny sun, like deep water.
And when all my brushes float in amber, when the easel's down,
and this work is within its frame, let these tired hands rest in yours.

—Isaac Timm

A CREATOR'S APPRENTICE

(Dedicated to the Player in us All: It happened in the Subtle Realms)

Robert Storey

Though I am Earth's God, yet often I'd slide away for reflection, remove myself to peacefully contemplate within the comforting folds of Nothing. Or, as my earthly charges had recently discovered—and quite appropriately named—that region of voidless anticipation where sentience is born, Dark Matter forever energized by Darker Energy.

This time, though, my other reason for dissolution into this nether region had more to do with a vague feeling of uncertainty. If I were still embodied, one could swear it was nothing more than déjà vu and I, now more than I had when ensconced in that coarsest realm of life, knew there was no such thing. Similar events are merely bred from similarity in deed.

Herein this vastness was a comforting limitlessness to and of space and time; herein—now I could measure the progress of those multitudinous aspects demanded by assignment over the past two millennia. How now those sentient beings within my controlling purview had risen, wisely I believed—though oft their chosen tracks "their goings on" did at times concern me—along the shadowy ladder of Everlasting Ascendance.

If a being such as I could really ever be prideful—correspondingly joyful!—as having been chosen by Our Universal Creator, these special moments melded in Nothing was just such a time.

When the Milky Way Director, Galaxy, was informed by the Creator of my selection as SheHe's resident choice for overall management of Sol's Solar System, there was, as expected, minimal dispute as to my abilities by HeShes throughout Now-and-Then-and-Forever. Most pleasing, nary a twitter of argument arose from those half-a-trillion or so other solar system managers within our nebula itself.

As one of my earthlings had reasonably observed about Our Creator's righteous authority, that stewardship without peer, "How can you really argue with the Boss?" Putting it plainly, as had they, this was the first Subtle Realm lesson I learned about hierarchical acquiescence.

The Chain-of-Commanded was explicitly outlined to me at the very moment of my earthly demise by dearest Galaxy: "It all begins at the top: Our Creator was, is, and will always be the One you will ultimately be responsible to; next, a step down the ladder of existence, there is I, and I am the being to whom you're directly answerable—My charge is this Galaxy, the Milky Way. Simply then, there comes you; beneath you are those mindful, sentient creations within the confines of Sol."

Immediately thereafter, the learning curve of being a God, so to speak, was not a curve at all! It was an explosion of immediate understanding. "A bolt from the blue!" was a quite applicable analogy, though the phrase itself as overworked as any earth-borne cliché could be.

As mentioned, these and similar thoughts were the typically blissful recollections upon which I dwelled during times when melded into Nothing.

Suddenly, surrounding these pleasantries, Galaxy intruded using ethereal embodiment.

"Our Creator wasn't happy at the Universal Conference of Creators' All.

"The criticism heaped upon SheHe was specifically of our robust life-directing activities: 'Ill advised!' said the Sixty-Four-eyed representative from Dimension Sixty-Four.

"Creator (Incensed? Playing at irony? I don't see how any of these terms could be applicable, so accentuated, by One-So-Glorious, but I did sense some odd inflections in HeShe's comments on the matter.) remarked, 'It's as if Sixty-Four's mega-eyed disturbance was waiting (eternally?) for us to blunder...just had to stick their umpteen noses in, wouldn't you know.'

"Again, I won't say Creator was ranting. A better way to describe the Chosen-One's words would be, stressfully adamant: 'SheHe, Sixty-Four's representative Know-It-All, decried our activity on one existential plain in particular; Earth was depicted as most distressing!'

"'Absolutely unconscionable,' Creator continued, 'how Sixty-Four repeated, and repeated, and repeated, those and similar charges; heaping accusations upon selective methods of castigations, etc. I add, punctuated, it seemed—and placing it on the scale of Everlasting-No-Start-No-End—*ad infinitum*. And that's putting it— pardon My overuse of earthly clichés, so catchy, they are!—mildly!'

"'Change the rules,' was demanded at the conclusion of arguments on earth's sentient viability, and this by the vast majority of attendees! I was told—would you believe 'told!'? —to correct the situation before another single millennia dwindles into dark matter! The whole business was reinforced—Stressed too, in particular, I should say, no less than by the Core Council on Life Progression.'"

As the voice of Galaxy's Essence-From-Nothing spoke, I shuddered. (The shuddering bit? Was that another slovenly trait I'd

91

somehow picked up from our creatures on that, that—now my most worrisome endeavor called earth? I wonder?...)

Being so indirectly directed directly by the Omniscience Rep of our Universe, it troubled me that something I personally had done was the direct cause of Creator's seemingly distressful (distressing?) commentary.

I kept silently mum, just listened—no use sticking your present personality—and, especially, your career—out there to get chopped to bits. Appearing outwardly nonplussed, within I diverted my vision back to the Big Bang; not wholly distracted, I recalled how it all began those many, many long light years ago.

"So SheHe's, Our Beloved Creator, decided you are to make some minor changes—maybe even a few majors ones along your path—in our goal-operations on each and every human-kind individual ASAP. Even if you must travel backwards into Earthly Everywhen.

"Don't worry, this won't affect your position rating or anything like that. But, just as an aside, I think Creator's going to give your assignment a bit of a jostle.

"I know you're trying hard to look upon this whole issue as a mere and, hopefully, minor intrusion on your grand plan for Earthly Ascension.

"Let me smooth your ruffles somewhat: you put your best essence forward and do well on this, and I'll bet your reward very soon will be a Universe of your own to initiate, monitor, and control. Say sometime, I would guess, within the next 100,000 years at the most."

Though still apprehensively silent, I felt it time to respond. It was that, or continue my stupidity-ploy of abstractness. "What's this 'minor change' thing? I sure hope it isn't to alter the prevalent planetary language. Mastering earth's dominant, prevailing languages over the ages have not been easy, you know. The last time going from understanding and speaking Russian to that hammered lingo American-English was a big pain in my you-know-what."

Galaxy hesitated a moment, then said, "I'll leave it up to you, since you're the Intern assigned the overall Earthly evolutionary chore."

I relaxed. Pulling my thoughts back into Now, I asked, "Could it be that my molding earthly affairs from afar's simply not worked? Guess a more hands-on approach's what's needed, eh? What do you think?"

Galaxy's essence was nowhere and everywhere. A trick, oddly enough, one I'd taught this superior of mine about the same time those earthlings discovered energy without substance, that elemental-existing from and in they-knew not-how-or-why-or-where. Then why Galaxy's sudden stillness? One all the more accentuated by Void?

Was Galaxy, both the He and She parts blended, purposely ignoring my question? It seemed so.

As quickly, the next words flew out of the blue, "One of the first things Creator directed me to do was...."

Again hesitation? "Go on. I can take it."

"Well...." Why was Galaxy acting like one of my earthlings? Afraid, oddly, to get to the point.

"Your title's being changed."

"What!?!"

"Creator obviously knows that over the 200,000 earthly years since SheHe's creation of woman/man on Earth, when moments—eons, I should say, after he lifted you to the status of Apprentice Creator, instead somewhere over the vastness of ages along the way you've changed...even more, they, your Prime Earthly Intelligence, has gone amuck!

"Rather than just your playing the role of absentee manager—I'm sorry, those words of Creators' did seem a bit snarky

93

even to me—you've taken up the lifestyle of the very creatures your Internship's directed you to direct!

"Don't get me wrong: Creator's not saying you've been lax or lazy. But HeShe's reasoning is, as expected, a lot more ethereal than that. I suspect, sometimes it's difficult even for One-Who-Knows-It-All to resolve a multi-faceted problem into a single point for minute reflection.

"In particular, SheHe never was enamored by your methods of human-enlightenment. Acts much too free—'Wandering, out of control,' was Creator's explicit emphasis, 'for humankind to rise in the ranks of Universal Sentience.'"

I suddenly felt as if I verged on the precipice of a total Galactic breakdown, if not a Universal one.

Crumbling, utterly distressed, I implored, "Does this mean what I think it does? How *must* I change?"

I sensed Galaxy's weakness; sadly—glaringly spot-lighted by Its present demeanor to me, at least—unable to take direct responsibility to discipline an underling. Even to and for one who was simply an Intern; one in dire, special need of Universal direction.

"Creator requests you relinquish your title as Intern."

"Oh no!" I knew now how my earthlings felt when they spoke of the Sword of Damocles hanging over them. That Sword now descending mercilessly my way.

There commenced an enormously prolonged moment— Nearly Eternal? —that followed; within this meaningless eddy composed of "God only knows what," I felt as if myself and my Galactic-Omniscience hung anchorless, suspended in some vacuum of remotest space. Some Eternal Void, absent entirely of Mind Throughout.

"I didn't' think it was all that bad!"

"Maybe I didn't make Creator's point clear enough for you."

Recovering back into Now, I asked, "Well, then, what does HeShe plan to do; this demotion in title does appear to me as a demotion in fact."

Each time I speak it's as if I'm somehow provoking even a greater resonant distraction in Galaxy's ambivalence. The prolonged—ageless? —non-reaction to my plea for clarity was having devastating consequences on my reasoning powers; my judgment abilities were peaking and falling by the decade. A roller-coaster ride of emotion, my earthlings would call it.

I felt Creator's emergence into the ether all around. Sensed, too, Galaxy's simultaneous and (trembling?) vibrational response.

How humbling for us both!

"I've been listening in."

"Eminence, Intern's acceptance to Your request.... "

"Dear Galaxy, your arriving at-the-point needs brushing up. Maybe it's You in need of Universal-Resurrection?"

Absolute obeisance from my Supervisor, Galaxy, I noted, when direct response was typically, absolutely expected—Nay, demanded, I thought!

I learned quickly, one such as I should never think out loud.

"Intern?"

I, much as had Galaxy, withheld response. Amenability, I now totally understood, was called for. Wait, listen, heed! That's all one now reasonably needs to do!

"The matter is simple. And, simply, resolvable."

"Eminence?" *Shut your face!* I heard within myself one of my Earthly charges demand.

My thoughts overheard, Creator commented, "I must admit, now and then, those creatures do seem to know how to, at times, purport themselves."

All thoughts drained from me. It was time for total Omniscient Absorption.

"Good. Now you're not thinking. All for the best."

Feeling, feeling only.

"I've noted, sadly, I might add, the sudden, wild abandonment of reason by your humans. Especially since the time you've allowed their entry into what you and they together refer to as their Industrial Revolution. Then the Atomic Age bit; blasting themselves not only into molecules, as did their merely explosive devices, but into nearly uncountable, unrejoinable, unrecoverable atoms!

That in itself wouldn't have been too much to ask, if—that's the big one! —they hadn't immediately coupled it to their penchant for total, exterminatorial warfare! So superior, they thought of themselves; as if they knew nothing of those beyond their own selfish, physical realm."

I couldn't help myself: Here it comes....

"Too superior, too fast! The demand by all Creator's, including those dimensionally non-sentient: Remediable action; remedial repair; remedial—Damn, you know what I'm getting at!"

Back to thinking, all I could say was, "Yes, Creator."

"To clarify. It *began* with their uppityness. It didn't bother me when some of the medical types—not shamans, those whom for ages and ages were intuitively anchored to a common, pastoral good—began to refer to their apprentices as Interns."

"I'm not sure I understand."

"Doctors in waiting! Interns! Is that not what they started to want to call themselves?"

Agreeing, "Agreed."

"Simply snob appeal."

I began to see where all this might be going.

"I want you, in particular you yourself, to back up in time and change this, preferably at the point where it all began to run awry."

"Good God!"

"Thank You!" A joke in there somewhere. "Maybe we should all go back then-and-when—even Myself—Great suggestion! From now on, it's permissible to refer to Me using that old-fashioned word used long ago...when and since time immemorial."

"Creator?"

"God. Creator's still okay...along with those other terms like HeShe and SheHe."

Here it comes. "Specifically then?"

"You. Your earthlings. Everyone needs to come down back to Earth, so to speak." Still that hint of humor?

"By?"

"Oh, let those apprentice doctors go ahead and still call themselves Interns. But for the rest...."

"Everyone else back to being called Apprentices?"

"On the Mark. Right on the head. Now You're finally using the old bean that I, God, gave you."

I hadn't rolled the old title—that once given me long ago—around my proverbial tongue in ages.

"Go ahead. Give it the old college try."

"Apprentice Creator." It slid across my mind easier than one might expect.

"Now that wasn't too hard, was it?"

I took HeShe at Their word, "Not bad at all...God."

"That was easy too, wasn't it?"

Added comment unnecessary; again time to remain still.

"Alright, that's over with. See how it's done, Galaxy?"

Galaxy merely grunted Its Ethereal Acquiescence.

Throughout the Universe there was Universal Calm.

Then, matter of factly, Creator spoke, "By the way, Apprentice."

"Yes."

"Have you picked anyone to succeed you when and if I desire to make your ascension a reality?"

My entire being joyously leaped through the Cosmos. Transported entirely by my happily exploding Mind.

Calming, I returned to Now to respond to God's request: "I've discovered a likely candidate 'Apprentice', Creator."

The three of us enjoyed the flavor of my remark.

"And who might that be?"

"A blended couple."

"A *blended couple?*"

"Well, it was the male's idea to begin with."

"How does that go?"

"He's a bit of a tinkerer, an inventor, of sorts. I overheard Gary—that's the fellow's name—express to his spouse, Corrie, that he'd just received a Patent Approval for one of his earthly inventions.

"And while they were gleefully engaged in discussion on his remarkable discovery, he said to her—jokingly I think—'For all my hard work I should at least expect a new title. One much more appropriate than my Geological Internship categorization."

"I know where you're heading."

The Void was immersed in a heady realm of laughter.

"'Corrie, dear,' Gary said, 'I've thought of a newer, more down to earth, wholly respectable, more appropriate title.'

'What would that be, dear?'

'How does Apprentice Creator sound?'"

More Universal laughing. A brief silence. Then the Creator-of-It-All spoke: "Now there's someone I can finally relate to. Good job, Apprentice!"

I inflated my world with pride...but not too much.

PARASAILING ON ACAPULCO BAY

Okay, okay, i'm clinging
to the darn shrouds--lifeline to boat below--
so small, I'm so big--legs dangling out at the sides--arms
straight up like arrows--hanging on by skin of my feet--fingers numb--
too much weight--slow down slow down--don't look down--don't--damn i did it--
i'm going to faint--water looks
cold--i'll make a big spash--glub glub--can't
hang on--have to interrupt lives--appointments--borrow money
for trip--arrangements--hang on tighter--oops--changed directions--those
idiots on the boat--whyohwhydidieverdothis--stop--stop--reel me in--can't you see im
in trouble morons-- can't
hang on much longer--man oh man--that first
kiss you gave me--rocked my world--gardenia corsage--we
danced-- danced--i'm slipping--just us--am i screaming or is it that big eagle--
don't attack--please--i had my head on your shoulder--one two three--one two three--
okay--that's it--she seduced you--
you'll be sorry when i die--i remember that
sandy beach where i danced in moonlight--all alone--nice--
can't you see me--legs dangling like big a X in the sky--I'm going to
drown--wonder how it feels--don't bury me at sea--put up a big monument--not a slab--
put a big fish on it--hope they're
happy--whoever sent me up here--gee-sand
has little crystals in it--ohnoohno--i'm going down--ouch--i'm
down--they're yelling at me--plowing up sand with my heels--keep head up--
i made it--i'm alive--hey out there sunning on your beach towels like nothin's happening
i made a perfect three-point landing and--
YOU DIDN'T EVEN SEE IT!

—Irene Hastings

101

DAWN OF A NEW MILLENNIUM—DAY ONE

Tim Keller

January 1, 2000, found me and a small group of friends ringing in the New Year at the Crystal Hot Springs Resort in the hills of Northern Utah. It was a special evening in more ways than one. Yes, it was the first night of the new millennium, but more importantly we had finally managed to convince my friend Mark to join us.

Everyone else changed clothes quickly, and they were already making the pilgrimage through the cold to the warmth of the pool. To prevent his escape, I waited patiently for Mark to get changed. Already he was carping from behind the door of the dressing slot, which was clearly filled to capacity.

"Look at this place," Mark grunted. "It's filthy! God only knows why I let you talk me into this."

"You'll feel better when we get outside," I soothed.

"Why?"

"You won't be able to see the filth."

The door popped open to reveal my less-than-amused friend in a stylin' pair of denim shorts, likewise filled to capacity.

"Not a word," Mark huffed as we walked into one of those crystal clear nights only extreme cold can bring about.

Mincing carefully to avoid the patches of ice that lined the pathway, we maneuvered through the darkness and settled at last into the steam-covered water.

Squeals of delight wafted over the resort. Seconds later, some teenagers half-ran, half-danced back to our pool.

"Oh, cool," I said. "The slide is open."

"You couldn't get me down that thing on a dare," Mark growled.

"Why not?"

"Just couldn't, that's all."

"Wait, you've never been down a water slide, have you?

No answer.

"How can you get to be thirty-five years old without going down a water slide?"

"Lots of people haven't."

"Yeah, in Afghanistan."

I know it sounds silly—grown men arguing over a water slide—but that's the nature of our friendship. I remembered the day Mark and I had met. I'd seen him around, of course, but we met at a training retreat where they made us play one of those ridiculous time-wasting ice-breaker games corporate trainers are so fond of.

Our hostess smiled like a predatory kewpie doll.

"Mark," she said, "I want you to tell Tim something about yourself. Something he didn't know before."

Mark furrowed his brow, as though he were deep in thought. "You know," he said, "I've never liked you."

The room held its collective breath,

"That's all right," I told him. "Who are you?"

"Come on," he pressed. "You know me, don't you?

"Well, I know everyone calls you 'Mr. Clean'."

"Oh, because I have OCD, right?"

"No, because you look like the guy on the bottle, but the OCD thing—that's interesting."

The tension broke and a friendship was born. It's like that sometimes; two overbearing people collide, and then connect.

Mark's response snapped me back to the pool: "I spent my time on more intellectual pursuits, thank you."

This simple deflection told me all I needed to know. Mark was afraid. Hard to imagine a man the size of a tank afraid and—in fairness—he usually isn't. But with his OCD, given the right set of circumstances, Mark is the elephant terrorized by a mouse.

Just getting him to the pool, a non-chlorinated public pool, and in the dead of winter, was a Herculean task on both our parts, a fact that I should have accepted and been grateful for, and I would have, really. Except for, well, his "intellectual pursuits" comment. That was a mistake for which he had to pay.

"It's okay if you're afraid—"

"I don't see you on it," Mark snapped.

"At least I have done it," I reminded him. "I liked it, I was very good at it and, most amazingly of all, I didn't die."

"Well you're too fat, now."

And the fight was on, escalating until the words "I dare you" were uttered. And suddenly, we were ten. See, the thing about guys is, regardless of how mature we seem, we never really grow up.

That's how, on the first day of the new millennium, my best friend Mark and I found ourselves side by side, huffing like a pair of locomotives up the tunneled stairs leading to the top of the water slide at Crystal Hot Springs Resort.

Steam rose from the warm water, sprayed from pipes along the walls to keep ice from forming on the steps. Kids raced around us as though we were merely monolithic obstacles placed there for their amusement. Their demented giggles wafted back through the steam, creating a distinctly creepy air.

When at last we reached the top, the arguing began anew.

"You have to go first," I said.

"I'm not going first. You go."

A steady stream of teenagers made their way around us to dive into the slide.

"You wanna go like them?" I asked. "They're going for speed, and they'll never wait for you. I, on the other hand, will."

The logic of my argument was unassailable and so, a buoy released from its anchor, Mark drifted lazily into the darkness. Steam rose from his body like smoke from a Viking funeral ship. I knew I was in for a long, cold wait.

And wait I did, forever, really.

"Come on mister, its cold," the kids behind me protested. "He's far enough—please? If you're scared, let us go first."

That last roused a part of me I thought long dead.

Scared? Mister? I'll show them scared. I'll show them mister. I was blazing down water slides before these little shits were born.

I grabbed the bar over the hydro-tube's gaping maw and swung into the slide like Tarzan from a vine.

I neglected to consider that, what serves as a toy for kids (and adults of lesser size and greater maturity), becomes the watery equivalent of a suicidal bobsled run for persons of "substance." The sensation of hurtling danger brought back my childhood. Never had I gone so fast, not for years had I felt this free. Yet through it all I could hear an inarticulate something.

"Stop!" Mark's voice echoed into clarity. "I'm stuck."

And as often occurs just before a horrific accident, time slowed down.

"Stop stop!" Mark screamed again as I whipped around the bend. "I'm stuck."

Now, Mark is an intelligent man, brilliant even. In spite of his panic, I saw the realization in his eyes—his denim shorts anchored him to the slide like Velcro, and we were going to crash. Even so, he made a valiant effort to escape, paddling with both hands like a wounded seal on Shark Week.

For a moment, just one, I was hopeful. If Mark could get out of my way in the half second he had remaining, whales could un-beach themselves, penguins could fly. Heck, Nessie might even be real.

Alas, the laws of physics would not be denied. All I could do was coil my legs into my chest on collision, then hurl Mark into the darkness.

That's when I heard the hoots and squeals, and felt a rush of water from upstream. I realized, that while I had waited patiently for Mark, the kids behind us gave no such consideration. I leaned back to accelerate, only to find Mark run aground again.

"Get your ass in the air!" I shouted. "Get your ass in the air!" My voice reverberated through the hydro-tube. "Heels and shoulder blades! Heels and shoulder blades! *Get your fucking ass in the —*"

Wham! The impact of a teenage body cut off my wind, and the impact of several behind him drove me ahead like a gunshot, straight into my bewildered friend. This time, he did throw his butt in the air and blazed away like a scalded cat, but the staccato concussion of several small bodies launched me ahead and yet again I was closing in.

Mark looked back as we reached the end of the slide. He appeared to accept the inevitability that the moment he exited the slide, I'd land right on top of him.

However, when he dropped from sight, I threw my legs up, leaned backward, and somersaulted over him, our combined water displacement triggering a tsunami that washed away the boys sitting on the edge of the pool.

Disheveled but otherwise unhurt, we made our way back to the therapy pool, the subject of many a curious glance.

ANTISEPTIC

Hot nurse with such light scrubs
lay your healing hands on me.

At sixteen, I'm all goose-bumps
with my bare feet and gown.

Hot nurse leans over, smells
of lilac—not nurse but doctor.

I'm embarrassed, such a crumb
to assume all women nurses.

Hot doctor with such light scrubs
lay your healing hands on me.

She does her tests, with a rubber
hammer, then warm hands in mine.

Testing my strength, my power;
how well I can push and pull.

Adolescent, male, Becker's, MD.
No noticeable change since last.

She smiles, with her perfect teeth,
coyly over note page, and leaves.

I feel warm and flush, I kick up
my feet, almost knock over a tray.

She comes back in, very grave.
She has caught me, now punishment.

Looking to her right, to see if we are
alone, and then comes in unsure.

All those teeth again, but no follow
through to her deep green eyes.

Then she blurts out: I don't know if
this has been addressed to you,

but it would be unwise for you
to have children. Then, pausing,

there are no changes to your health
that I've found. Here's the attending.

From the right comes the boss doctor
in his long coat so crisp and white.

He smiles at her, approving of a hard job
so well done by a young intern.

She does not look back, just leaves.
In her path: lilac over antiseptic.

—Isaac Timm

THE YELLOW DUCK

Emily Younker

The yellow duck bobs in the water. I sink low. The water barely teases the bottom of my nose as I blow out my mouth. The bubbles from my flapping lips send the duck into another spin. I can never get him to fall over.

"Robert, are you done yet?" my older sister asks.

The water in my bath is room temperature, the cue to get out. Mom never likes it when we take too long. Four children, two parents, a cousin, and a visiting family friend limit bathroom time. I scoop up Mr. Duck—I named him when I was only three—and dry off. With the towel around my waist and the duck in hand, I leave.

I keep the duck with me so my younger sister won't play with him. She nearly broke him a couple of weeks ago. Made his squeaker blubber. Dad only fixed him because I was in tears. I never cry.

"No self-respecting nine-year-old would cry over a duck," he murmured. "Would you like a matchbox car? How about some army men?"

I took the repaired duck and left. Mr. Duck has an honored place on my shelf. Dad still grumbles whenever he sees it but never does anything. I rarely see him do anything.

Technically, everyone else in the family had ducks. Everyone but the little destroying monster who always gets into my stuff and wrecks it. She wasn't born yet when the package arrived on the door step with enough ducks for everyone in the family. A typed note lay on top.

"Please use daily. Thank you."

Each house in neighborhood received a box and a note. I know because everyone still talks about it. There was no trace of where the boxes came from or why. Some people threw them out immediately, some of them talking about governmental plots. My family brought the ducks in. I immediately took one out and named it. My older sister and brother fingered them and said no thanks. I think sis said it because brother did. She always tries to imitate him.

All the ducks in the city are long gone, except mine. Actually, I think Krissy down the street still has one, but I don't really know. Neither of us mentions the ducks because they aren't cool.

Sometimes men in black suits come into town but they're always thrown out. They talk about the city being dangerous, or something. Even I know that's a lie. I sometimes wonder if they left the ducks and that's why people hate them. Whenever something odd happens or there's a new car in town, it is the government's fault.

With Mr. Duck safe, I go outside. The trees are bare, but everyone hopes the leaves will come back soon. It's warming up. I don't know when the leaves are coming back and I don't care. Doesn't change my life whether they're here or not.

Since school's out, there's not much to do. Mom and Dad are always working or sleeping. My sisters are always busy in their rooms, and even my cousin, who moved in a couple of years ago, rarely leaves the house. Mom says it's because of the machine. The way she says it makes me laugh. I've seen the machine; it's nothing more than an old boxy computer. I use to watch him play, but Mom found out and made me stop.

We have a guest staying with us but he only sleeps here. I heard Dad complaining to Mom that we weren't a hotel and they were either going to get paid or the friend could find another place to live. The friend came, the friend stayed. Dad always loses the argument against Mom. I once asked the friend what he did. He explained something regarding something. It has a long name and I don't understand. I don't ask for an explanation. People like him always talk a lot and never make sense.

I wander down the street with my hands in my pockets. There are only a few people on the street. Most of them move slowly about their yards. A few wave. I wave back. I see a car down the street at Krissy's house. A neighbor scowls at it and mutters under his breath.

No one answers at Henry's house. Henry's my best friend. More of my third-best friend, but Steve and Charlie are sick. I'm Henry's fourth-best friend, so it works out. I like his house. His mother always offers chocolate chip cookies. I don't know who doesn't like being here.

I try knocking again and press my face up against the glass. A figure moves slowly to the door.

"Robert," Henry's mom says. She coughs a couple of times, then adds, "I'm sorry but Henry can't play today."

My face falls and I mumble my thanks. I jam my hands in my pockets and kick a few pebbles as I walk back to my house. If Mom and Dad find out Henry's sick, too, they won't let me go back over. Once my friends get sick I'm banned from their house. That's the reason school's out. Too many sick kids. At first it was fun, not having school. Not anymore. Now there's nothing to do. I spend the rest of my day in my room. Mr. Duck watches me read a few books and color.

I help set the table for dinner. Only two plates, Mom and me. The rest are eating dinner in their rooms. It's been this way for a while. Some nights I'm the only one who eats at the table. Someone knocks on the door.

"Get that, Robert," Mom says.

"Sure." No one ever comes to visit me anymore. I wonder if Henry is feeling better.

Two men in black suits stand on the step, looking down at me. They are definitely not Henry. I can see the car from earlier behind them, parked on the street.

"Robert?" one of them asks.

I slowly nod, taking a step back.

"You need to come with us."

"No, thank you," I mumble and try and shut the door.

"No," the man says, grabbing my arm. "There's no time, the filter won't help anymore."

They pull me off my feet. Kicking does no good. My mom only watches through the window, her face blank like she doesn't even understand what's happening. I cry and scream but no one comes. In the back of black car, Krissy looks at me through red, swollen eyes. We drive out of town. A man pounds in a large sign as we go by. Do Not Enter. Contaminated.

The first tree we pass is completely covered with leaves.

OBLIGATORY ROSE POEM

If roses have hips then
shouldn't they have feet
that pound in swift
needle heeled stiletto
tempo on tile, a straight
forward here-she-is stride
that makes a man stand up
and pay attention,
an echo that demands eyes
all the way up the stem
to a figure well fit into
tailored red coat.
Bobbed hair, short skirt
creates the movement
That drives a man to write a poem.

—Isaac Timm

ALL THE WESTERN STATES

Chadd VanZanten

Sarah came from one of the big, rectangular states out west. Colorado or Wyoming. I could never remember which one because the one I thought was Colorado is actually Wyoming and the one I thought was Wyoming is really Montana. It didn't matter. You could say she was from all the western states, that her state of mind was western. That's what first attracted me—she was miles of open space.

I once told her the cookies she baked tasted like damp cardboard from a pizza box. That was the first time she ever got angry with me. I think it was the part about the pizza box that tipped the scales. I thought it was a nice touch but, apparently, Sarah believed that pizza boxes were constructed of some lower species of cardboard, and bringing their kind into an argument was hitting below the waist.

We'd been together for almost six months by then. Most of the other girls I knew had been angry with me several times before we even went out. Not Sarah. It took uncommon effort to make her angry. This made me suspicious, of course. I assumed it was a sign of serious emotional problems, or some plan to make me look foolish. I was disappointed to learn it was neither.

She said, "Why get angry? Anger makes you bitter."

I said, "Yes, I'm aware of that. Trust me. I know how to be bitter."

We first met when she moved into the apartment across from mine. One day at the beginning of the semester, she said hi to me in the hallway. Naturally, I assumed she wanted to borrow something, or get directions to Harris Hall, but she really only wanted to say hi. I'd never known anyone who said hi to strangers for the sake of it. It was a custom I'd heard of, something society once accepted but now deemed a little dangerous, like candles on a Christmas tree.

"Where I'm from," she said, "that's what we do. We say hi to be nice."

"Where I'm from," I said, "when someone's nice it usually means they're getting ready to rob you."

"That's so sad," she said.

Not only did she mean it, she was right. It was sad, something I hadn't thought of until just then.

"You should come to the game with us later," she said, as though this might serve as consolation for my entire childhood.

"I've never been to a football game," I said.

"Oh, then you've got to come," she said, clutching my coat sleeve, shaking me. "We're gonna win!"

She was right about that, too. The Wildcats always won with Sarah in the stands. I imagined the players on the field would somehow spot her in her matching hat, scarf, and mittens, her nose and cheeks red.

In the huddle the quarterback would say, "Did you see her? That country girl in section F?"

They'd all nod, breath smoking out from their face masks.

"We gotta win this thing," he'd say. "Win it for her."

She was just that elegant. Not evening-gown elegant, but elegant like a sailboat, like she'd been designed in some flash of

120

genius. The short, straight hair. The high cheekbones. Genius. There will always be men to win games for Sarah, not just to earn her love, but simply because she exists.

Unfortunately, that sincerity, that raw authenticity comes at a price. For example, her favorite movie was "The Lion King." She didn't know what gnocchi was, or tapas. She liked Kraft macaroni and cheese.

"Don't laugh," she said, pouring out the electric-orange cheese powder. "Where I'm from we don't try to get fancy, but we always eat as a family."

"Where I'm from, we only do that when somebody dies."

"That is so sad," she said, and she meant it.

That's what made her special. That was her super power— she meant every single word she said. I didn't just hear Sarah talking, I could feel her talking. When she had something important to tell you, she'd hug you first. Or she'd tell you while she was hugging you. When she grabbed me and whispered, "I'm falling in love with you, Charles," well, it was (as they say out west) big medicine.

She moved in with me. I watched "The Lion King" with her once, and I even ate the macaroni and cheese she boiled up in my $300 Mauviel copper saucepan. I assumed after I made her my quinoa-and-gouda salad, and we watched a few Fellini films, things would change, but the western states, the really big ones, are farther than you think.

One time she said, "Another French movie?"

I came back with, "Sorry, they didn't have any 'Little House on the Prairie'."

But she was impervious to that sort of acid. "Oh, really?" she moaned. "Dang. I love that show."

When I took her out for Latin-Thai food for the first time, she said, "Why do you keep taking me to places where I can't read the menu?"

I said, "Because I wasn't sure what kind of wine goes with a broccoli and cheese Hot Pocket."

"Me either." She shrugged, eyes wandering over the menu. "Maybe just a wine cooler?"

The subject of butter put even more miles between us. In my opinion, you can't cook without real butter, let alone bake. Sarah never touched it. She used something called "I Can't Believe It's Not Butter," which, by the way, really must be the most presumptuous product name ever.

That's what ruined her cookies. The recipe called for butter, and this wasn't butter. It was like an artist's conception of butter, by a not particularly talented artist, an artist who has only heard stories of butter.

Sarah's mother used butter substitutes exclusively when Sarah was a kid out west. Apparently, margarine was a way of life for folks of that generation, though whether this was a cost-saving measure or a dietary concern I never found out. Either way, it wasn't entirely Sarah's fault that she preferred I Can't Believe It's Not Butter, which, by the way, really ought to come with some kind of abbreviation, if for no other purpose than to assist couples who are arguing about it. It's impossible to make a point when you have to say that whole name every time. I suggested we shorten it to "It's Not Butter" since that's the one part of the name which is actually true. Sarah didn't think that was funny.

The thing that was truly hard to believe was that someone from out west could lead a largely butterless existence. I could understand learning to tolerate and maybe even becoming accustomed to butter substitutes after eating it all her life at home, but I couldn't see why she kept eating it after she moved out.

"Your mother's not here," I said. "How can you use that fake butter when there's actual butter right next to it in the refrigerator?"

"It tastes more buttery."

"Sarah," I said. "Nothing can taste more like butter than butter."

"I never said it tastes more like butter," she said. "I said more buttery."

"Same thing," I said. "Butter is, by definition, the most buttery thing there is."

But I could already see her next move, and she saw it, too.

"That's not true," she said after a pause. "Sugar is more sugary than a sugar beet. Altoids are more minty than real mint. Right?"

Of course she was right. But now I needed to know what it took to hurt her, if anything could. Besides, I'd never lost an argument to her and I wasn't about to let the first one be about margarine. As I considered how long it would take her to find a new place and move out, I held up her sad little cookie and hit her with the cardboard remark.

"This is like biting down on wet cardboard from a pizza box. It's vile."

That slowed her down. I won't say it stopped her in her tracks, but she felt it. She folded her arms and looked at me with an expression that made it clear she considered me the injured party in the matter.

It didn't break us up. We had much bigger fights than that and stayed together. I'd be surprised if she remembers what I said about her cookies back then. She didn't move out until a few years later, and I don't believe it was my fault in the end. She graduated, for one thing, and then moved to Arizona for grad school. Or New Mexico. I forget which one—whichever one is next to Texas.

Sarah unfolded her arms and moved close to me. She took the cookie from my hand, tossed it in the trash, and said, "Where I'm from we just don't say things like that to each other."

"Where I'm from that wouldn't even be considered a real insult."

"Charles," she said. "That's just sad."

I said, "Yeah, you're right. But so am I."

She nodded, gave me a hug. "Then I forgive you," she said.

She meant it, and that's what really hurt.

THINKING LIKE PABLO

I will speak with a hummingbird,
I want her to build me a place
that defies the wind, that rocks in a gale.
Then I shall talk with an eagle…
I'll borrow his sight for
I am old and my eyes darken.
I will look to the meadowlark
for he will sing my childhood
back to me.
Yet I seek the deer's wisdom
for he always knows danger.
I want to talk with a star to learn
where he found his light years…
I want to ask the roses to flower
all year, the rain to bless earth
on signal, to kiss a cloud
in its descent, to forgive
nature's violence.
And when these things are done
I will search for God…

—Marilyn Ball

THE GIFT

Tim Keller

Mom usually begins her Christmas shopping in June, but this year she announced she would no longer buy presents for all the children, grandchildren, and great grandchildren. Instead, she would take down Dad's life story and use the installments as gifts for the family.

Secretly, I and everyone in the family considered this something of a holiday foul, but the folks are long retired now and as the family has grown, the time and expense of shopping for everyone has gotten prohibitive. So, we all smiled and nodded politely.

Only I suspected the truth—that Mom would nag Dad until he finally deigned to speak. She would then write his every utterance in longhand until her arthritic fingers could take no more, and leave the resulting hieroglyphs for me to decipher.

When she brought me the notebook to transcribe, it was all I could do not to groan. Except for a list of titles ("My First Horse," "My Trip to the Dentist," "The Old Yellow School House"), the pad was empty. I realized that, in addition to my own holiday and writing responsibilities, I could now look forward to—this.

Mom must have read the frustration in my expression because the next words out or her mouth were: "Your father is a great man."

It's a familiar refrain. What's more, it's true. Stalwart and glacially calm, his moral compass reliable as true north, Dad's an exemplar of his generation, but though I love him dearly, we've rarely seen eye to eye.

Dad was born a middle-aged conservative who took his seat on the high council the moment he left the womb. I, on the other hand, am impulsive and ruled by passion. We get along all right around other people, but alone, we're sort of like two old tomcats circling in an alley.

"I know," I assured her. "It's just, do you want to write it down for me?" I asked hopefully. "Then, I could, you know, edit it. That way, it would sound like Dad was doing the telling."

"No," said Mom, "I want you to give it some style. You know, write it like one of your books or something."

Wonderful, I thought, pulling out my laptop. *The gift that keeps on taking.*

"Yeah," Dad said with an amused snort. "Style me up."

"Dear," said Mom in that special tone of hers, the one that says *proceed at your own peril.* "Dear, I know you think this is silly, but it will save us over two thousand dollars in gifts this year alone. So, you can take this seriously or you can break out the checkbook and start writing."

I started up the laptop, sat on the sofa facing Dad's chair, and waited smiling. Mom had us trapped and we knew it. Dad grunted a begrudging affirmative, cleared his throat and began to speak.

I grew up during the Great Depression and my family was large, even by the standard of the day. Then again, people didn't worry about things like that back then. Yes, more kids meant more mouths to feed, but they also meant more help around the farm. Families took care of each other in those days, you see.

With four older brothers and four older sisters, I was the baby of the family. Which meant that Mother and my sisters spoiled me rotten, while the older boys had to do the heavy farm work. The only bad part was that everything I owned used to belong to someone else! I got two new pairs of pants a year—a church pair on Christmas and Levis for school on my birthday. Everything else was a hand-me-down, including my horse.

Buttons became mine by default. She was too old to carry anyone else in the family, but I was only six years old at the time. I couldn't lift the saddle to put on her, nor could I reach her head to bridle her, but to the family's amazement, I could call and over to the fence she'd come. I would give her some oats, climb the fence, slip onto her back, and off we'd go.

This went on until my mother saw. That's when Papa, (at Mama's insistence,) taught me how to wrap a rope around Buttons' head and neck. Just like that, I was the only boy in all of Mink Creek with his very own horse. She would take me over Devils Hill to Grandma Christensen's for a cookie, or over Jensen Hill to the hot springs with my buddies.

We were just little kids but folks didn't worry like they do today, and our parents all knew—old Buttons looked out for us. Like the time my friend Arlen told us they had baby geese at their place and we should all come see. His daddy told him to stay away from them, but they were only geese. So, we rode Buttons over to his place and slid off her to see the geese.

"They can already swim," he told me.

Of course I didn't believe him. Surely they were too young.

"They can," he insisted. "Help me chase 'em to the creek and I'll prove it."

So, we rounded 'em up and were headin' 'em to the creek when the mother geese turned and came at us. Their necks were craned forward, wings outstretched, and they honked so loud it hurt our ears. The lead one flew up, grabbed my nose and beat me with its wings. I started screaming. I thought they were going to kill us.

Old Buttons came charging to the rescue. Her first pass sent geese and feathers everywhere. She stood between them and us and reared up, beating the air with her hooves. It was an awesome sight for us little kids.

The geese beat a hasty retreat and they were the last geese I ever bothered. Word got around that Buttons had saved us and we were famous.

She was as faithful a companion as a boy ever had, but as I grew up, her coat grew spotty and she developed a deep bow in her back. As a pure-bred quarter horse, she'd once been the fastest in the territory. Now she could barely lope. Buttons was still a great friend, but she just wasn't fancy to a bunch of eleven-year-olds no longer afraid of geese, (not much, anyway).

So, Buttons and I went from famous to infamous, though anyone who said as much could (and often did,) end up with a black eye, and much as I loved her, even I had to admit she was an old nag. I begged my father for another horse, a real horse, maybe even a thoroughbred. But it was the Depression. We had work horses and Buttons. My brothers had to ride the Clydesdales, Dad reminded me. He said I should be grateful and I knew he was right. If I wanted a horse of my own, I would have to think of a way to get it myself.

I wracked my brain trying to figure that one out. I was heartsick. I had five dollars saved up, but I wanted a horse like the one I saw at the county fair that summer. The old Johnson ranch got foreclosed on that year. A California dude bought it at auction and started trucking in livestock. The first time any of us ran into him was at the county fair, where he showed up with King, the most magnificent horse I'd ever laid eyes on. Horses like that went for hundreds of dollars or more, even in those days.

King was an enormous white stallion, both good natured and fast! He passed all the locals like they were standing still. What with my appreciation for fine horse flesh, seeing that animal made it all the worse. There was no way I could afford even a regular horse, much less a magnificent steed like him. I was already doing all the work I could fit into a day, doing chores and hauling hay at home, then doing odd jobs for the neighbors.

I worked and prayed, prayed and worked and, as always happens when you do your part, inspiration came.

That night at dinner, I asked Papa, "If I can find a way to get my own horse, can I keep him?"

My brothers all laughed at me and I turned red, but I was determined to have my answer.

"Sounds fair to me," he said, as Mama hushed my brothers up.

I set to work the very next day.

The Anderson family owned a big dairy back then and, in fact, their land bordered the old Johnson ranch. This was before milking machines, and the cows had to be milked twice a day. No one wanted to work at the dairy. It was hot and dirty work, especially in the summer. So, when I asked Mr. Anderson if he needed any help, he hired me on the spot, leaving only Mama to convince. She seemed to sense the urgency of my need and, to my great surprise, even let me out of church for the whole summer.

It was hard work, all right. Every day I rode Buttons over to Anderson's before first light and led her up the hill to the pasture.

It wasn't too bad in the morning. The cows would be waiting patiently by the barn door, and the family of cats we'd give the occasional squirt, lined the wall. We'd run the cows in, two at a time, milk 'em, dump the bucket in to the milk cans, run 'em out and do two more. I'd go back up between milkings to get Buttons, ride home exhausted, do my chores there, and then ride back up.

The afternoon milking was a different story. We had to fight the cows, the heat, and the flies. Even the cats'd be gone. The hotter the day the thicker the flies, and when the cows couldn't swish them off fast enough with their tails, they'd head for the creek and run through the brush to get 'em off. Then Buttons and I'd have to ride down there and drive 'em back.

Come Friday, I'd get paid five whole dollars for the week. I was too tired to ever spend it and it wasn't the money I was after, anyhow.

Fall rolled around and back to school and church I went. Every morning I rushed through my chores so I could sneak Buttons some extra oats, apples, and carrots from Mama's kitchen.

By Thanksgiving old Buttons had a certain glow about her. By Christmas she was downright fat, and my brothers Glenn and Nathaniel, the businessmen of the family, were suspicious. One day they stood by the pasture fence, arguing about whether Buttons could be pregnant, vying for the colt just in case she was.

"She's my horse" I reminded them.

"I'm older," Nathaniel told me. "You can have my Clydesdale."

"Hell, that horse ain't pregnant," Glenn opined. "She's just fat."

"Thing's ready for the glue factory if she ain't," Nathaniel said.

That made my blood boil. My plan, all my hard work—I could feel it all slipping away. Much to my shame, my eyes started to water.

"It's my horse and my colt!" I declared.

"What you gonna do, baby boy? Cry?" Nathaniel asked, and shoved me away.

We were taught to love each other, and we really did, but ashamed as I am to admit it, at that moment I hated him.

"She's mine!" I screamed, jumping on his back.

Nathaniel was seventeen and real strong, but I wrapped my legs around him, sank my teeth into his neck and held on for dear life.

He shook and bellered until Papa came and pried me off.

Nathaniel jumped up and looked to come after me, but a single, particularly expressive snort from Buttons bought me a head start. I ran screaming into the house and hid in my room. Mad and embarrassed, Nathaniel gave chase, but Mama met him at the door while my eldest sister Helen followed me to my room.

I broke down and told her the story; how I'd rode Buttons over to the Anderson's in the mornings, and pastured her right next to the old Johnson place. Once there, I simply unhooked the fence wires to let Buttons in with King.

The look on Helen's face made me suddenly very nervous.

"What?" I asked. I'd grown up on stories about how they shot horse thieves on sight. "She had to eat too, didn't she? It wasn't stealing, exactly. I mean, King was the one who took care of business, after all."

Helen laughed, and I knew I'd be okay.
"Before long, Buttons had a boyfriend," I told Helen. "And when she started kicking at King a few weeks later, I knew the deed was done."

Helen called Mama, and I'd just got through relating the story to her when Papa, Glenn, and a bloodied-up Nathaniel came in.

"Why did you bite your brother?" Papa growled.

"Adam Archibald Keller!"

My mother rarely called my father by name, and in all my life I'd never heard her use all three; it certainly got his attention.

135

"That horse is his and that colt is his! You gave him your word, and that's one promise I aim to make sure you keep!"

Not to be outdone, my father shouted, "Has this whole danged family gone nuts? Good hell, woman, that thing's 'bout as pregnant as I am."

You could hardly blame him. It's not every day you see a twenty-five-year-old mare on a farm full of geldings catch pregnant. Talk about Immaculate Conception.

"Then you'd better stock up on saltines and hot towels," Mama said, "because Leness has a story to tell you."

By the time I was done, order was restored and everyone was in good spirits. Everyone but Nathaniel, anyhow, and even he settled down, eventually.

Papa made me go see Mr. Johnson, who'd stayed on the land as the ranch foreman. I admitted what I'd done and had to work for him every day of Christmas vacation, but I didn't mind.

On a blustery April afternoon, Buttons gave birth to the most beautiful little philly I've seen before or since. Very light palomino with a star on her head and four stocking feet. Between me, Buttons, and my sisters, no horse was ever loved more. The girls called her Kate, but being a boy, I named her Skyrocket.

Buttons died peacefully a couple of years later and Papa died of cancer a year after that. The sale of Skyrocket's foals helped us keep the family farm. Years later I said a tearful goodbye to Skyrocket as we sold her to pay for my mission to Georgia. Mama never told anyone, but she put what she didn't use in savings bonds and when I got back from Korea, she cashed them out to help with my first house.

I typed furiously, trying desperately to capture the moment, when I realized the room had gone quiet. Only the whir of the fan on my laptop and the ticking of the clock could be heard. I looked up to find Dad staring off into space, his eyes moist.

"Wait, Skyrocket?" I asked. "You called Queenie Skyrocket, and Kate before her."

"Every horse since Buttons," he said. Then he picked up the newspaper and I could tell we were done.

I gazed at him like a stranger. There sat my father, an old and honorable man, to be sure, but for the first time, I also saw a twelve-year-old boy, sneaking his ancient mare through a fence.

www.ingramcontent.com/pod-product-compliance
Lightning Source LLC
Chambersburg PA
CBHW071350170626
46811CB00003B/1074